HINDUISM
ANCIENT AND MODERN
VIEWED IN THE LIGHT OF THE INCARNATION

HINDUISM
ANCIENT AND MODERN
VIEWED IN THE LIGHT OF THE INCARNATION

BY

JOHN A. SHARROCK, M.A.
PRINCIPAL OF ST. BONIFACE COLLEGE, WARMINSTER
MISSIONARY IN SOUTH INDIA (1877-1909)

GYAN

Published by

GYAN

Gyan Publishing House
5, Ansari Road
Daryaganj, New Delhi-110002
Phone: 011-47034999, 9811692060
E-mail: books@gyanbooks.com

Distribution Network
gyanbooks.com
India, USA, Canada, UK, Australia, France

ISBN : 978-81-212-2154-2 (PB)
First Published, 1913

2nd Impression 2021

Printed at: Gyan Press, Delhi.

Hinduism
Ancient and Modern
Author: John A. Sharrock

HINDUISM
ANCIENT AND MODERN

VIEWED IN THE LIGHT OF THE INCARNATION

BY

JOHN A. SHARROCK, M.A.

PRINCIPAL OF ST. BONIFACE COLLEGE, WARMINSTER
MISSIONARY IN SOUTH INDIA (1877-1909

Society for the Propagation of the Gospel in Foreign Parts
15 TUFTON STREET, S.W.

1913

PREFACE.

THE World Missionary Conference, held at Edinburgh, was not only an inspiring experience of a lifetime to those who had the privilege of taking part in it, but it was an outward symbol of an awakened zeal and of a new spirit of union, which was catholic both in its scope and character (at least one eminent Roman Catholic Prelate expressed his sympathy with the objects of the Conference) such as would not have been possible at any previous period in the history of Christendom. One important lesson of the Conference was the need of a more extensive study of missionary problems on the part of those interested in the extension of Christ's kingdom. If this need is to be met, an increase of our missionary literature must take place, and the literature which already exists must be revised in the light of the increasing knowledge of the missionaries who are engaged in the work abroad.

The number of Hindus who are well versed in

English literature is daily increasing, and the Eastern and Western nations are daily being drawn closer together. Not only do Indian Christians read the works of English theologians, but Hindus are keenly interested in various branches of English literature. Still, both Christians and Hindus are far too apt to ignore the study of the religions of their own country —the former from a perhaps not unnatural feeling that, as they have discarded Hinduism, they may neglect the scientific study of that religion; and the latter from a thirst for all the new knowledge which the West opens out to them. But, on the other hand, as India is in a state of mental and spiritual, as well as political, turmoil, and as tens of thousands of Indians are consciously or unconsciously turning wistful eyes towards Jesus Christ as the greatest religious Teacher that the world has ever known, and, perhaps, as the only Teacher who can solve their doubts, any book which honestly places the two religions side by side must be of assistance to them in their perplexities. It is the author's hope that this little book may be of as much use to Hindus searching for the truth as to English Christians anxious to understand the religion of their fellow-subjects. Nothing less strong than the bond of a common faith can bind the two races together in sympathy and brotherhood; and the closer the approach the closer will be the tie.

Some English readers are ready to dismiss the whole Hindu religion as so much "heathen superstition," whereas others go to the opposite extreme, and, ignoring the dark—and it is a very dark—side of Hinduism, revel in it as in a sublime philosophy. In these pages an attempt has been made to treat the whole subject as fairly as possible, but there has been no shutting of the eyes to the hideous vice of Krishna or the obscene rites of the Tântric orgies.

Another matter of great importance is the study of Comparative Religion on the part of students preparing for their examinations in our Theological Colleges. This subject is almost entirely ignored even in Missionary Colleges—like the one with which I have the honour to be connected—for a general education and special preparation for missionary work are hard to combine. We have no choice in the matter, for we are bound hand and foot by the usual theological examinations. We teach Latin, Greek and Hebrew, but know nothing of Sanskrit, Arabic or Chinese. We are well versed in Gnostic heresies, but know nothing of the *Vêdânta* or the three *Pitakas* of Gautama. We could safely meet an Arian, but should be dumb in the presence of an Âryan. We can discuss the doctrine of the Unity in Trinity, but cannot point out the fallacy in the creed of Islam that "There is no God but Allah," or in the Hindu's conception of the Trimûrtti. And the same line of argument applies with scarcely less force to other Theological Colleges and other Divinity examinations.

He who knows only Christianity, but is ignorant of what millions of other people believe, does not really know Christianity. Let the usual foundations be well and surely laid, but let us test those foundations by seeing how they will bear attack from non-Christians; and let us not rest satisfied with mere foundations, but go on to build on them an impregnable fortress standing foursquare to all the world. We shall never learn to think clearly, nor shall we teach precisely about the dogmas of our own religion, till we have studied them in the light of the other great religions of the world.

If asked what is the object of this small book, the author can perhaps answer best by imitating the negative methods of the sages who wrote the *Upanishads*. When they were questioned by their disciples as to the nature of God, "Is it this?" or, "Is it that?" they almost invariably replied, in their dread of binding down the Deity by human limitations, "*Neti*," "*Neti*," "Not so," "Not so". Is this, then, a book of original research? *Neti*. Is it a translation of, or commentary on, the sacred books of India? *Neti*. Is it a history, or scientific exposition, of Hinduism? *Neti*. The sage thus reduced his conception of God to that of bare existence. This book, it is hoped, contains something more positive. It is an attempt to grasp the main features of Hinduism, both higher and lower, both ancient and modern, both theoretical and practical; and then it is an endeavour to compare these features with the central dogma of Christianity on the part of one who has spent the best years of his life as a missionary in India.

It is an attempt to bring both ancient and modern Hinduism within the purview of that large body of men and women who are now interested in Missions, but who have no time to study difficult books on Hindu philosophy and mythology, and no opportunity of examining Hinduism on the spot as a great, living and many-sided religion in the way that a missionary has. The latter must not only study the sacred books of the East, but must compare their teaching with the religious beliefs which he finds embodied in the lives and customs of the people.

A scholar engaged in original research must confine himself to the written documents; whereas the working missionary has to deal more with men's hearts, and with their lives, thoughts, customs and observances. So great is the divergence between theory and practice found to be, that the missionary would be tempted at times to throw aside his books altogether, were it not that the "mighty maze" of conflicting opinions and the innumerable observances of modern Hinduism are "not without a plan," and are only rendered intelligible by being co-ordinated with the teachings of the ancient sages. The field of Hinduism is so vast and the jungle so dense, that ordinary readers are often repelled from any serious effort to explore and penetrate them. It is difficult to see the wood, in fact, for the trees. There are not many people who care to plunge into such an entanglement of mighty trunks smothered with masses of luxuriant creepers and the undergrowth of shrubs and thorns; but there may be some who will be glad to be guided along the main tracks where they may take note of the various plants and gorgeous tropical flowers, and perhaps identify some of them as belonging to the same genus as those which they have seen in our own quiet woods and well-ordered gardens. There are many books on Hinduism, but for the most part they are long and difficult, and are so loaded with details as to defeat their own ends. If this small book has any value, it will be due as much to what it omits as to what it includes. In selecting the materials for use there has been no attempt, I repeat, at originality. It is not necessary for a builder to make his own bricks, but it is sufficient if he builds his cottage according to his own design. There is an abundance of excellent material available, and I have not hesitated to make use of such as I have needed for the present purpose. On the Hindu side I am chiefly indebted to the Rev. W. Dilger's book on *Salvation in Hinduism and Christ-*

ianity[1]—one of the most trustworthy books that I have read, and Prof. Max Müller's *Gifford Lectures.* On the Christian side I have largely followed Dr. Illingworth, Bishop Westcott, and others who are the recognized authorities on such subjects as the Personality of God and the Incarnation of our Blessed Saviour.

It may be thought that we have books enough of this kind, but a distinction must be drawn. Our library shelves are laden with works on the different doctrines of the Christian Faith, which contain references to the various non-Christian religions of the world. It may, however, be of no less profit to take the main facts of one non-Christian religion and place them, so to speak, in parallel columns with the corresponding dogmas of the Christian Faith. We have not too many books of this stamp.

Again, the question may be asked, is not our Christian theology too much a theology of the past? The study of Comparative Religion has scarcely commenced with us. Yet we are now in contact with every race on the globe; our problems are not those of a defunct past, but such as deal with the living creeds of living races; we cannot waive those beliefs aside as mere heathenish superstitions, for we are confronted with the most abstruse philosophers, and are opposed

[1] I have availed myself of the author's kind permission to make use of his book wherever necessary.

by scholars of repute. Must we not begin to live less in the past and more for the present and the future? There are other languages besides Hebrew, Latin, and Greek. Some day we shall have to burst the bonds of our insularity and parochialism; become catholic in our claims and views; and cease talking of "foreign" missions as "extras". Some day we shall realize that Christianity is face to face, and in deadly conflict, with the great religions of the world—to conquer or be conquered. We shall find that the forces arrayed against us are the greatest of all forces; and that the problems we have to solve, such for instance as the caste and race problems, are those most difficult of solution. When we have grasped these facts, we shall realize that the creeds and problems of living races demand the best intelligence of our theologians, as well as the systematic study and self-sacrificing devotion of all Christians.

CONTENTS.

I.

INTRODUCTION.

ERRATA.

Page 71, line 20. For *removing* read *rearing*.
" 77, " 2. For *our* read *on*.
" 132, " 14. Omit *human*.
" 179, note 1. For *Hinduism as a Social System* read *Missions to Hindus*.

to the Greeks. When they entered India, and settled in the neighbourhood of the Hindu Kush many centuries before the Christian era, they were as much foreigners as we English now are. Their gods, the "Bright Ones" (*Dêvas*, compare *Deus*, Θεός, Divine, etc.), were for the most part the gods of nature, and their religion was distinctly polytheistic. After the *Vêdic* period came that of *Brâhmanism* and the *Upanishads*, when the sages evolved their marvellous philosophic system, after searching into the very depths and caverns of human thought, and endeavoured by the aid of their own efforts, unassisted by Divine revelation, to discover the Supreme Essence, the Absolute Self. Then about the sixth century B.C. arose the great

I.

INTRODUCTION.

MOST people who have read anything of what is called Hinduism are aware that this religion is divided broadly into three periods: ancient, mediaeval and modern — polytheistic, philosophic and idolatrous. Before the old Âryans split off from the common stock they spoke the same language and worshipped the same God as our own ancestors. God was to them, speaking generally, the Sky-Father (*Dyaus Pitri*), as he was Jupiter to the Latins and *Ζεὺς Πατήρ* to the Greeks. When they entered India, and settled in the neighbourhood of the Hindu Kush many centuries before the Christian era, they were as much foreigners as we English now are. Their gods, the "Bright Ones" (*Dêvas*, compare *Deus*, Θεός, Divine, etc.), were for the most part the gods of nature, and their religion was distinctly polytheistic. After the *Vêdic* period came that of *Brâhmanism* and the *Upanishads*, when the sages evolved their marvellous philosophic system, after searching into the very depths and caverns of human thought, and endeavoured by the aid of their own efforts, unassisted by Divine revelation, to discover the Supreme Essence, the Absolute Self. Then about the sixth century B.C. arose the great

(1 M./O. 17390)

reformer Gautama, the Buddha, the enlightened one (born 557), waging war against the gross forms of sacrificial and ritualistic observances then practised by the Brâhmans, and against the degrading system of caste. In their desire to maintain their supremacy the Brâhmans adopted two methods; first, persecution of the Buddhists in the cruellest manner, and secondly, the development of Krishna-worship, which appealed to men's worst animal passions and served as a counter-stroke to the austerities practised by the followers of Buddha. The two systems were in deadly conflict for some centuries, and Buddhism was finally vanquished: but just as in the parallelogram of forces the body acted upon no longer moves along either of the sides but along the diagonal of the parallelogram representing the two forces, so Brâhmanism was entirely altered by its struggle with Buddhism in its trend of thought.

Next, when we come to consider the lower form of Hinduism which is held by the great mass of illiterate Hindus in the present day, we shall see that it is both a survival of religious beliefs long anterior to the Âryan invasion, and also a strange medley of superstitious observances, tinged, to a greater or less degree, with the Brâhmanic philosophies of the predominant caste. When the Âryans entered the country they did not find a clean slate as regards religion any more than we Christians have done. The Drâvidians who had settled there before them had blended more or less with the aborigines, and each had learnt from the other, something of animism, blood-sacrifices, fetishism, magic, idolatry, devil-propitiation, and witchcraft. The Brâhman missionaries were satisfied if they could persuade the people to call their idols by the names of their own gods; to associate their own religious rites in some way, however slight, with the Brâhmanic philosophy and ritual; and, above all, to adopt the system of caste by which they themselves were considered to be God's human representatives, while the Drâvidians and aborigines became graded under them according to their different ranks of caste or no-caste. If we can imagine some Roman Catholics settling down in Africa and making nominal converts, who still continue their old practices of fetishism and polygamy, and their old beliefs in witches and rain-doctors, while at the same time accepting the Pope as the infallible representative of God upon earth, then we shall have some faint idea of the Hinduism held by the bulk of the illiterate Hindus.

It is here that the difficulty of the Christian missionary chiefly lies. It is easy for him to master the various books on Hinduism, of which some are excellent and others unreliable, according as they are written by men who are, or are not, acquainted with the language of the common people. As soon as the missionary is capable of talking familiarly with all classes of the people, and has learned the actual conditions of their lives, he will discover that their religious observances are widely different from what he has read in the books. He will find himself surrounded by a perfect maze of conflicting opinions and contradictory observances, and he will also be left very much to himself to grope his way in the dark. It is only by actual experience that he can learn the practical side of this difficult work. This book is but a small contribution to the study of Comparative Religion; but it is hoped that the experience of one who has studied the philosophy of the sacred books, lectured to the higher castes in College, preached to the illiterate folk in the villages, and discussed Hinduism in all its bearings with all classes for over thirty-one years, may be of some use to others, whether missionaries or students, to make them acquainted with the main lines of thought, to help them to avoid the numerous pitfalls, and to give them a clear, if only a bird's-eye, view of the whole subject. I have not, however, thought it necessary to give a complete dissertation on either Hinduism or the Incarnation, but have rather tried to show where the two come into contact, and how they are contrasted. But this contrast leads us, if I am not mistaken, to the very core of both religions.

It is hoped that this small book may also be of some use to Hindus who are seeking after the truth. There are many thousands of educated Hindus whose minds are unsettled. In spite of desperate efforts to galvanize the old Vêdism into life, and to allegorize away such parts of the Hindu scriptures as shock the newly formed moral sense, and in spite of the foundation of many reforming societies and eclectic religions, the Hindus can find no rest for their souls. They are proud of their philosophic system, evolved by their subtle-minded sages—a system so deep, so exalted and so logical as to have won the admiration of world-famed scholars. But is it not possible for us to explain to them the only true sense in which the Supreme Being is the One God, though not One-without-a-second; and show them how the Incarnation of Jesus Christ is the only solution of their great problem about personality either in man or in God? Again, caste is, and always has been, an almost insuperable stumbling-block in the path of the Hindus. Were it not for caste, tens of thousands of educated and high-caste Hindus would to-morrow become Christians, as they themselves admit. Can we not point out to them that Christianity contains within itself a brotherhood infinitely higher and nobler than any caste system? The human brain can conceive of no grander union with the Supreme than that attained by all those who in Holy Baptism have been made "sons of God". Nor can the human heart long for any joy sweeter than the communion with God, the Immanuel, in the second great Sacrament, when these same "members of Christ," while retaining their individual personalities, become one with the Son of the living God. No one who seriously compares the bliss of those who have the gift of eternal life and the hope of heaven with the misery of those who are always striving "to cut short the eighty-four lakhs" (8,400,000) of births, to end finally in an unconscious absorption in an unconscious Essence, can for a moment hesitate in his decision as to which is the happier lot.

CHAPTER I.

THE NATURE OF GOD IN THE VÊDAS.

POLYTHEISM.

TO understand Hinduism aright we must begin at the beginning, and give a very brief description of the rise of the religion with the adoration of individual gods; and sufficient quotations from the *Rig Vêda* to illustrate the same, and to reveal to us the minds of the ancient Rishis (sages) who wrote the earliest poem. Part of the Vêdic religion was no doubt hereditary and belongs to the Indo-Germanic period; and part of it was absorbed from the cults of those who had settled in India previous to the Âryan invasion. We shall see this action upon, and absorption of, other cults vastly increase as we descend step by step from Vêdism to Brâhmanism, and from Brâhmanism to Hinduism as we now know it.

When the Âryans[1] settled in India they looked upon the splendour of the encompassing sky and spoke in awe of their Heaven-Father (*Dyaus Pitri*), and then as they beheld this sky embracing on the horizon the

[1] The first â must be pronounced as in "father," so as not to confuse the Âryans with the heretical Arians.

ample bosom of Mother Earth, they prayed for the blessing of the "Great Parents," "Heaven our Father, Earth our guileless Mother" (*Rig Vêda*, VI. 51, 5). These, like husband and wife, became the progenitors of the other radiant deities (the *Dêvas*, or bright ones) and were thus addressed:—

"I praise with sacrifices mighty Heaven and Earth
At festivals, the wise, the strengtheners of law;
Who, having gods for progeny, conjoined with gods,
Through wonder-working wisdom bring forth choicest boons".

(*Rig Vêda*, I. 159.)

Again, we have the idea of the goddess Aditi associated with the Sky-Father. She, according to Max Müller, is "boundless space," and from her is evolved the same idea of heavenly progeny. Of their sons Varuna (perhaps οὐρανός) is the first and chief. He is the king and creator of the world, and is not only the protector of men but the avenger when the moral law has been broken. It is he with his mares, Phœbus-like, who keeps the path of the Sun-god unimpeded and loves to dwell in the pleasant places of heaven and earth. It is often said that the gods of the Vêdic period are mere personifications of nature, but this is not entirely true, as will be seen below. Again, though it is true that these gods are manifestations of "power" as distinguished from love, virtue and gentleness, one of the chief functions of some, like Varuna, is to preserve the laws and to guard the morals of mankind.

Another sun-god is Mitra, a name which carries us back to Mithra, a Persian god, with whom the Âryans must have been associated in the pre-Vêdic period, in fact some centuries before they entered India. Mitra was also another god distinguished for moral attributes. These gods are very different from later ones such as Indra, revelling in war and intoxicated with the Soma-juice.

The following beautiful verses may be quoted as specimens of the delight of the earlier gods to dwell in the house of righteousness, to punish evil and to invoke blessings on the devout:—

(5) "For these, even Ayaman, Varuna, Mitra,
Are the chastisers of all guile and falsehood.
And these, Aditi's sons, infallible and mighty,
Have waxen in the home of Law Eternal.

(11) "He who wins favour for his prayer by worship,
That he may gain him strength and highest riches,
That good man's mind the Mighty Ones will follow:
They have brought comfort to his spacious dwelling.

(12) "This priestly task, gods, Varuna and Mitra,
Hath been performed for you at sacrifices.
Convey us safely over every peril,
Preserve us evermore, ye gods, with blessings."

(*Rig Vêda*, VII. 60.)

It will not be necessary to dwell on the features of all the thirty-three Vêdic deities—since expanded into thirty-three crores, or, 330,000,000—but it will suffice to give brief notices of the chief gods, and to mark their characteristics.

Sûrya (ἥλιος, *sol*) is the sun-god, with whom Varuna and Mitra are associated. He drives his seven mares through the sky, revealing with his bright rays the good and evil in men's lives:—

> " His bright rays bear him up aloft,
> The god that knoweth all that lives,
> Sûrya, that all may look on him ".
>
> (*Rig Vêda*, I. 50, I.)

Savitar is another god associated with the sun who stimulates all life and movement. The fervid orb causes seeds to germinate, and draws up the luxuriant vegetable life from the damp earth, and hence Savitar as the stimulator becomes also a sun-god. This deity is chiefly of note because it is in connexion with him that we have the famous prayer called the Gâyatrî. This prayer has been offered for the past three thousand years, and is still chanted by every devout Brâhman morning by morning, as he raises his joined palms to the rising sun in adoration.

> "Let us meditate on the adorable light of the divine
> Ruler (Savitri);
> May it guide our intellects."
>
> (*Rig Vêda*, III. 62, 10.)

Ushas (ἠώς, *aurora*) is the goddess of dawn, "nobly born, the daughter of Heaven". Like a young and beautiful maiden she shines brightly, "stirring to motion every living creature".

"Turned to this All, far spreading, she hath risen
And shone in brightness with white robes about her.
She hath beamed forth lovely with golden colours,
Mother of kine, Guide of the day she bringeth."
(*Rig Vêda*, VII. 77, 2.)

Two of the most prominent gods, to whom a large number of hymns are addressed, are Agni (*ignis*), the god of fire, and Indra; the first representing the sacred fire of the sacrifice and the domestic hearth, and the second the Indian Thor, or Hercules of antiquity, and also, in his capacity of the thunder-god, the counterpart of Jupiter Pluvius. It is Indra who slays Vritra, the dragon that had enclosed the waters in his castle prison. He it is, also, who destroys with sudden and ruthless attack the godless Dasyus who performed no sacrifices—probably Drâvidian and aboriginal races.

"He who hath smitten, ere they knew their danger,
With his hurled weapon many grievous sinners;
Who pardons not his boldness that provokes him,
Who slays the dragon, He, O men, is Indra."
(*Rig Vêda*, II. 12, 10.)

The war-god needed to be stimulated with the intoxicating Soma-juice, which was known in the early Indo-Iranian period, and was called "Haoma" in the Avesta, and was the ambrosial nectar of the gods of ancient Greece and Rome. This drink, which was poured out as a libation at sacrifices, became itself worshipped as god. The following lines, supposed to be spoken by Indra, illustrate well the stimulating effect of the draught on the god, and form, in fact, a kind of drinking-song:—

"This, even this, was my resolve, to win a cow, to win a steed:
Have I not drunk of Soma-juice?
Like violent gusts of wind the draughts that I have drunk have lifted me:
Have I not drunk of Soma-juice?
The draughts I drank have borne me up, as fleet horses draw a car:
Have I not drunk of Soma-juice?
The hymn that reached me, like a cow that lows to meet her darling calf:
Have I not drunk of Soma-juice?
As a wright bends a chariot-seat, so round my heart I bend a hymn:
Have I not drunk of Soma-juice?"

(*Rig Vêda*, X. 119.)

Another Vêdic god is a strange gigantic being who is described as follows:—

"A thousand heads hath Purusha, a thousand eyes, a thousand feet.
On every side pervading earth he fills a space ten fingers wide.

This Purusha is all that yet hath been and all that is to be;
The Lord of immortality, which waxes greater still by food.
So mighty is his greatness; yet, greater than this is Purusha.
All creatures are one-fourth of him, three-fourths eternal life in heaven.

(*Rig Vêda*, X. 90.)

According to the myth this primeval being is sacrificed by the gods, and out of his members are made the different powers of nature, such as the sun out of his eye, and the wind out of his breath, etc.

This list may be closed with the names of two other gods, Rudra and Vishnu, who are included not because of their importance during this period, but because Siva—with whom Rudra is supposed to be associated —and Vishnu are the two chief gods of the present day. The modern Hinduism of the orthodox may be roughly divided into two sects, those of Vishnu and of Siva. It may be mentioned in passing that the origin of Rudra is given as a post-Vêdic legend, when an entirely different set of religious ideas prevailed. According to these later writers that origin is the basest conceivable. The gods wished to avenge themselves on Prajâpathi, the creator of the world, for an act of incest, and so they "put all the dreadful things found within themselves together in one heap, and therefrom arose this god" (*Aitareya Brâhmana*,

III. 33). But the creation of this disgusting god led to very unpleasant results for human beings. To avoid his bow and arrows, and "all assaults of mischief," men called him Siva, "the auspicious one," somewhat in the same way as we say "good dog" to pacify the vicious cur that is snarling at our heels. Vishnu and Siva are also, according to later writers, the second and third persons of the Hindu Trimûrtti, the Trinity of the Hindus—Brahma the first person having practically dropped out—with which we shall have to deal later on. Vishnu takes two steps on earth and by his footprints provides "spacious dwellings" for "the humble people who trust to him for safety".

"Three times strode forth this god in all his grandeur,
Over this earth bright with a hundred splendours."
(*Rig Vêda*, VII. 100, 3.)

And the third step conducted him to some sacred abode of bliss to which even "the feathered birds of air" do not "venture to approach".

Enough has now been said to show the Vêdic conception of the Deity, and to prove that that conception is a distinctly polytheistic one, in which one god after another receives the highest conceivable honour from the particular sage who happens to be writing his hymn of adoration. It is also evident, as has been said already, that though nature-worship is the predominant feature, and power is the chief glory to extol, yet there are other conceptions which are not so materialistic, and which show that there are gods not lacking in ethic qualities, but who are worthy of being addressed in verses which contain much that is not only religious in the highest sense, but also poetic in sublimity of thought and gracefulness of diction.

In comparing Vêdism with Christianity and hence with the central doctrine of the Incarnation, it will suffice to point out that the latter is based on the great doctrine of the unity of God. It is only when we begin to study Comparative Religion that this doctrine looms out of the mists like some huge, immovable rock. When, for instance, we treat of Islam, we see what a tower of strength is found in the short clause, "There is no God but God"—the One, the Almighty Lord of heaven and earth. Were it not for this dogma which, of course, Muhammad learned from the corrupt forms of Judaism and Christianity prevailing in Arabia in the sixth century, Islam would be but a poor invertebrate religion indeed. Brought up, as we have been, from our childhood, with the Creeds always sounding in our ears, we do not perhaps realize at first the strength of the foundation on which our faith rests. Had we lived in the fifth century of our era, the words "The Godhead of the Father, of the Son, and of the Holy Ghost is all one" might have sounded like a trumpet call in our ears. Going back for another thousand years we might have realized how difficult was the task, from the days of Abraham to the Captivity, of preventing the Jews from falling into the error, from which none of their neighbours escaped, namely, of imagining that the Godhead can be divided up into a number of major gods and goddesses like Varuna, Indra, Ushas, and Vishnu, and minor gods innumerable. A careful reader of the Old Testament cannot fail to note the persistence of the cry of all their prophets, and how fatally easy it was for the Jews to slip back into the belief in gods many and lords many. Abraham was encompassed all round by tribal gods when he was taught by Divine revelation the belief that God is one. Then, again, his descendants had always reverberating in their ears the oft-repeated designation of the true God—"the GOD of Abraham, Isaac, and Jacob". This is one of the first great facts of revelation. As Max Müller says: "If we are asked how this one Abraham possessed not only the primitive intuition of God as He had revealed Himself to all mankind, but passed through the denial of all other gods to the knowledge of the one God, we are content to answer that it was by a special Divine Revelation".[1] The same central truth was once more impressed on the mind of Moses at the burning bush: "I am the LORD thy God . . . thou shalt have none other gods before me" (Exod. XX. 2, 3). And the clarion note is sounded forth, "Hear, O Israel, the LORD our God is one LORD" (Deut. VI. 4). Again and again the Israelites fell into idolatry and polytheism; again and again the prophet sounded the alarm, and punishment fell; till finally, in the misery of captivity at Babylon, they once for all renounced their idols and accepted the fact that God is not

[1] *Chips from a German Workshop*, p. 373.

manifold but One (Is. II. 8; Jer. II. 11), and so realized that this is the commandment which is the first of all (St. Mark XII. 28, 29). The faithful in Israel were thus prepared by painful steps for the advent of the Messiah, the key to all their perplexities; and may we not also see the Hindus, many centuries behind, being led by equally slow and painful steps to the foot of the Cross? "The Supreme Being cannot be multiplied; it is incapable of a plural; it cannot be a generic term."[1] In later chapters we shall see also how this Supreme Being must also be personal, and next, that the Incarnate Son is both the complete Man and also very God. "If the Father is God and the Son God, they are both the same God, wholly, unreservedly. God is a particular, and unique, not a general term. Each is not only God, but is the very same 'Singularis unicus et totus Deus'."[2] The Hindu denies personality in the Godhead as derogatory to the Divine Nature and knows nothing of such an incarnation as that of the Second Person of the Trinity; hence he has built up the amazing system of philosophy which we must now consider.

[1] Moberly, *Atonement and Personality*, p. 83.
[2] *Ibid.*

CHAPTER II.

THE PHILOSOPHIC CONCEPTION OF THE SUPREME BEING.

THE UPANISHADS.

LEAVING the Vêdic period we arrive at the second stage of Brâhmanism (800 B.C.—A.D. 1200), and must now consider the philosophic system as expounded in the Upanishads, which, far more than the four Vêdas, form the basis of the higher Hinduism. The word Upanishad means "sitting down beside," and so these works may be described as lectures listened to by disciples sitting round their guru, or perhaps as books of meditation.

The child races of the world turn to Nature and deify the sun, the rain, animals and trees, by a kind of instinct, as the visible symbols of God; but as soon as they begin to grow up and think for themselves, they long to find some Supreme Being in the infinite space beyond and behind all natural phenomena. The world has never known a race of deeper thinkers than these Âryan sages who have pushed thought to its utmost limit; who with their finite minds have groped after the infinite; and who with patient eagerness, and without the light of direct inspiration, have felt after God if haply they might find Him. Thus these Âryans turned from polytheism and strove to find a philosophic basis for the Divine. So many scholars have spent their lives in searching into the sacred books of the East, and in endeavouring to fathom the mysteries of Hindu philosophy, and have also placed the results of their research within the reach of all students, that it would be unprofitable to go over the ground again in any detail. Many of those who take a general interest in the mission work of the Church abroad, have neither the time nor the inclination to study these sacred books, but yet will be glad to get a bird's-eye view of the subject, especially in so far as it may be compared with the philosophic basis of Christianity.

Even during the Vêdic period (say 1500—800 B.C.) the sages began to look for unity in the Godhead, and realized that though there may be many deities such as Indra, Mitra and Agni, yet those gods are in reality all one.

"To what is One sages give many a title."
(*Rig Vêda*, I. 164, 49.)

The following hymn reveals in a striking way what a yearning filled the mind of some sage of old as he tried to fathom the mystery of the Great Final Cause and the origin of the universe:—

"Then there was neither Aught nor Nought, no air nor sky beyond.
What covered all? Where rested all? In watery gulf profound?

Nor death was then, nor deathlessness, nor change of
night and day,
That One breathed calmly, self-sustained; nought
else beyond It lay.
Gloom hid in gloom existed first—one sea, eluding
view,
That One, a void in chaos wrapt, by inward fer-
vour grew.
Within It first arose desire, the primal germ of mind,
Which nothing with existence links, as sages search-
ing find.
The kindling ray that shot across the dark and drear
abyss,
Was it beneath? or high aloft? What bard can
answer this?
There fecundating powers were found, and mighty
forces strove,—
A self-supporting mass beneath the energy above.
Who knows, who ever told from whence this vast
creation rose?
No gods had then been born—who then can e'er the
truth disclose?
Whence sprang this world and whether framed by hand
divine or no,—
Its Lord in heaven alone can tell, if even He can
show."

(*Rig Vêda*, X. 129, translated by Dr. Muir.)

Different sages have given different descriptions of the origin and nature of the Supreme Being, inconsistent with one another; and so it is not to be wondered at that different schools of philosophy have sprung up, varying so widely as to teach both Monism and Dualism, that is, that the Supreme and the universe are one, and also that they are two and distinct. According to the earlier Upanishads we certainly get the idea that the phenomena of the world possess some reality, whereas in the later books, Brahma is the sole existence, and the sole reality, while all else is an unreal illusion. "There is but One, no second" (*Êkam êva advitîyam*). This Supreme is known under different names, such as Brahma (that which grows, from *brih*, originally denoting the expansive force of nature),[1] and Parama Âtmâ (the heavenly Breath, the Soul, or the Self). Another name is Prâna, which comes from the same root "an," to breathe; and it is interesting to note how common is the conception that the breath connotes the life and inmost soul or self (cf. *spiritus*, *πνεῦμα* and רוּחַ). But perhaps the nearest designation, or description, of the Supreme is found in the compound word *Sat-chit-ânanda*, i.e. existence, intelligence and bliss. Before we go any further we must try to get some notion of this Supreme Self, or Brahma. Is It God? No, for our word God implies personality, and personality limits the Infinite by the finite. Is It Creator? Not so, for creation denotes conscious activity, while Brahma is neutral and unconscious. Is It Father, King, Redeemer? No, no. What, then,

[1] Cf. *Hindu Pantheism*, by Colonel Jacob, p. 2 n.

is It? We seem to reach something conceivable, if not tangible, when we say It is "Existence-Thought-Bliss". But even here we must be cautious. The Supreme Self does *not exist*, for as a primal germ It cannot exist, but It *is Existence.* It is also Intelligence, abstract thought without any object on which to display Its intelligence. Similarly, It is Bliss without an object of love, and so merely the negation of misery.

May we pause for a moment here to utter a word of protest? The ordinary matter-of-fact Englishman with his strong ideas of common sense and his practical views of everything in heaven and earth and sea, is apt either to ridicule Hinduism as a mass of gross superstition beneath contempt, or to treat with absolute indifference their philosophic systems as too grotesque and mystical for serious consideration. And he does not realize that he is himself in danger of blundering out of the spiritual world into rank materialism, and so of rendering himself an object of amazing pity to the orthodox Hindu whom he despises. Nor yet does he understand that his love of the practical, his dread of mysticism, and, above all, his reluctance to think things out for himself, often cause him to be strangely ignorant of the inner meaning of his own religion. Let us, then, while trying to ascertain the Hindu's conception of the Absolute Self, treat his views with respect, not only because they are worthy of it, but because such disciplined thought will give us a truer knowledge of the Godhead, and a clearer understanding of our own Christian Vêda—the word and revelation of the Divine.

We start, then, with the great fact that Brahma, the Soul, is self-existent, neutral, unconscious and impartite. The sages arrived at this conclusion by negative rather than positive declarations. We must try to appreciate something of their horror of anything that limits or curtails the majesty of the Supreme. To the Vêdântist God—and this term is only used in deference to Christian custom—is the sole existence: everything—or rather everything that *appears* to exist—comes from Him (or, It), and goes back to Him. But that was not the idea in the mind of the philosopher. He was simply striving to guard the Supreme Being from mundane and materialistic conceptions. He shrank with dismay from everything which savoured of anthropomorphism. Personality appeared to tie God down to human limitations, and worldly existence; and so the sage abandoned all ideas of personality, and conceived of the soul as unconscious, belonging to neither sex, and impartite. It was a small matter to him that this Absolute should be pushed further and further back till He became a Something unthinkable by the human mind; but it was of vital importance that He should be unfettered by the chains of humanity, should keep His majesty undefiled by anything material, and undimmed by the shadow of anything mundane. We can but admire the loftiness of their aim and the awe with which they dealt with this sacred subject, especially in the presence of so much irreverence, indifference and materialism among some Christians. Let us see, when we compare our own system with theirs, whether we can give a rational conception of Christianity, which neither passes beyond the limits of finite comprehension, nor lays us open to the charge of materialism or of derogating from the majesty of the Most High. To the orthodox Hindu the Christian is one who dwells on a lower plane, incapable of soaring to his own sublime heights, and who drags down the Deity by his personal conceptions to his own mundane level. To the Christian, the Hindu has stripped the Deity, in his dread of human limitations, of one attribute after another till he has reduced Him to the vanishing point and made Him a sublime Nothingness. Is it not possible to conceive the idea of GOD as a Being transcending in His power and holiness all human thought, dwelling in light unapproachable, and untrammelled by our limitations, and yet at the same time so near to us that we may call Him Friend—nay even Father—while we live in His Presence and enter into communion with him as His sons? He is infinitely above us, and it is almost inconceivable that we should have the high honour of being "sons of God"; but still the doctrines of the Fatherhood of God and the personality of man, implied in the term sonship, do not derogate from the awful majesty of the Most High.

Let us first look at the Hindu's conception of the Absolute Self in detail, and consider the Christian conception in later chapters when we deal with the

Personality, Immanence, and Transcendence of God. To imagine that any man or tree, worm or blade of grass is independent of Him, beside Him, or different from Him, is to curtail His majesty. To imagine that He has any personality like man is to limit Him, to subtract from His infinity, and so *ipso facto* to make Him cease to be God. To think that He has any attributes or qualities is to degrade Him to the level of man, or at least to that of a Divine Creator who is lower than the Absolute Self. I was once reading a leading article in *The Hindu*—the chief paper in the Presidency of Madras for Hindus—and came across these startling words, "The Hindus have never sunk so low as to believe in a personal God"—the very thing to which we Christians most firmly attach our hopes—Our Father, Who is in heaven. Now Hindu philosophy *does* find room for Prajâpathi—the Creator of the world—but it looks upon such a Creator as only a part of the Absolute Self, and in a lower and temporary stage, and one who must finally be absorbed in Brahma. This Brahma—the all-pervading Essence—is both neutral and unconscious, for consciousness, like personality, connotes attachment more or less close to the material world. It is void of all attributes (*nirguna*) and also of all moral qualities. To fathom the Hindu's idea of the Nature of God, and hence of the nature of man, we must briefly consider the mystic syllable A U M, pronounced ÔM. Each of these three letters taken separately and then combined as a syllable, corresponds with the four stages in the existence of Brahma.

The first sound, A, is the waking state of the soul, whether individual or Supreme, for the two are the same. The second, U, is the soul in the condition of dreaming sleep. The third sound, M, is the soul in a state of dreamless sleep. While the whole syllable O M "is that which knows not internally or externally (i.e. there is no difference between the subject and object of knowledge) . . . it is neither known nor knowing (for every trace of individual consciousness and memory has vanished); the invisible . . . the inconceivable, the thing without characteristic distinctions, the unthinkable, the unspeakable, that which can be reached only through the knowledge of the unity of Self. That which is the multiform universe is abolished; the calm, the blissful, the non-duality, that is deemed to be the fourth. This is the Self; this is to be known" (*Mandukya Upanishad*, I. 1, 7).

Thus the Self has no longer any trace of personality. It has become neuter, for It is an absolutely impersonal principle or entity—solitary, calm, motionless. This entity, which is the sum of all entities, can only be reached by the individual Self after the latter has, stage by stage, lost all consciousness, and has been ultimately swallowed up as a drop of rain is swallowed up in the ocean—an ocean of that which is only saved from being nothingness by being unconscious Existence. This fourth condition is the pure state of the Absolute Brahma, into which everything must return; and is even beyond dreamless sleep, so that self-consciousness is now quite out of the question. To the sages of the Upanishads it is the highest and most transcendental condition conceivable, because in it every shadow of self-consciousness is abolished. And it follows as a necessary consequence that an entity which has neither personality nor self-consciousness cannot possibly have any moral quantities.[1]

Having endeavoured to make the general idea plain, it may now be well to illustrate the text with a Vêdic hymn. The following hymn is not only a beautiful piece of poetry—and the general reader will be glad to know that the ancient sages of Âryavarta, like our own modern poets, could "sweetly make and sing"—but also shows how there was gradually evolved from the conflicting claims of many gods on man's adoration, the conception of one God without a second. It is called the hymn of "The golden germ" (*Hiranya-garbha*).

1. "In the beginning rose Hiranyagarbha,
   Born only Lord of all created beings,
 He fixed and holdeth up their earth and heaven.
   What god shall we adore with our oblation?
   (*Or*, To whom shall we offer sacrifice?)

2. Giver of vital breath, of power and vigour,
   He whose commandments all the gods acknowledge,
 The Lord of death, whose shade is life immortal.
   What god shall we adore with our oblation?

[1] *Salvation*, by the Rev. W. Dilger, p. 110.

3. Who by his grandeur hath become Sole Ruler
   Of all the moving world that breathes and slumbers;
He who is Lord of man and Lord of cattle.
   What god shall we adore with our oblation?

4. His, through his might, are these snow-covered mountains,
   And men call sea and Rasâ his possession:
His arms are these, His are these heavenly regions.
   What god shall we adore with our oblation?

5. By him the heavens are strong, and earth is steadfast,
   By him light's realm and sky-vault are supported;
By him the regions in mid-air were measured.
   What god shall we adore with our oblation?

6. To him, supported by his help, two armies
   Embattled look while trembling in their spirit,
When over them the risen sun is shining.
   What god shall we adore with our oblation?

7. What time the mighty waters came, containing
   The universal germ, producing Agni,
Thence sprang the gods' one spirit into being.
   What god shall we adore with our oblation?

8. He in his might surveyed the floods, containing
   Productive force and generating worship.
He is the god of gods, and none beside him.
   What god shall we adore with our oblation?

9. Ne'er may he harm us, who is earth's Begetter,
Nor he whose laws are sure, the heaven's Creator,
He, who brought forth the great and lucid waters.
What god shall we adore with our oblation?

10. Prajâpathi! Thou only comprehendest,
All these created things, and none beside thee.
Grant us our heart's desire when we invoke thee:
May we have store of riches in possession."
(*Rig Vêda*, X. 121.)

The word Rasâ, it should be explained, is a river in heaven, and Prajâpathi means the "Lord of Creatures". The general idea is, that this golden germ is the eternal principle of existence which created all other gods and the whole cosmos, and so is the basis on which all the system of philosophic Hinduism rests.

The Supreme is under one aspect known as Purusha, the primeval Spirit.

"This Purusha is all that hath yet been and all that is to be;
The Lord of immortality."

So the immortal gods and all human souls are summed up in, and derived from, the universal Spirit. In the atheistic Sânkhya philosophy we shall find below that Purusha, associated with *Prakriti*, or eternal matter, bases the universe on a dualistic system. Another idea, according to Deussen, is that Brahma, the Absolute Self, was evolved from Brahmanaspathi, the Lord of prayer, so that the power of worship and devotion during the sacrifice was made the principle of all existence, including Absolute Existence Itself. Still another conception is that relating to Skambha, the "pillar" of the universe which supports "existence and non-existence," i.e. existence and potential existence. The performance of austerities and sacrifice connect this "pillar" with the last idea of Brahma as the power of prayer.

It may here be noted that during the Vêdic period the neuter word *brahma* means "prayer," while the masculine word *brahmâ* stands for "priest". In the later philosophic period the neuter Brahma denotes the supreme Self or Soul, while the masculine Brahmâ is the Lord, or Îsvara, who becomes finally absorbed into the Self.

It should be noted, too, that the Brahma is imperishable and impartite, possessing no moral attributes (nothing but pure existence), without beginning and without end.

"The Self is not born, it dies not, it sprang from nothing, nothing sprang from it. It is for ever birthless, and has ever been so" (*Kath. Up.* I. 2, 18).

Again the Brahma is absolute Light.

"In that highest golden shrine lies the Brahma pure and undivided.
Those who know the Self know the brightly gleaming Light of lights."

(*Mund. Up.* II. 2, 9.)

We must not confuse this with the Christian idea of

God as the "Father of lights," for St. James (I. 17) not only meant that God, the source of all light, is higher than the sun, or any Sun-god, which owing to its revolution, leaves half the world in darkness, but is the Father of such "good gifts" as life, fertilizing clouds, and worldly prosperity; and also of those "perfect boons" such as the conscience, eternal life, the indwelling of the Holy Spirit (or *Átmá*), and so on. Brahma has no ethical attributes and so is only the light of the intellect. The Upanishads lay no claim whatever to, but rather disavow, any *moral* attributes in the Brahma. For we read:—

"Really these thoughts do not arise to the Self: 'I have committed sin, I have done good'. It is superior to either; It is not affected by what It has done or by what It has not done." "It is not defiled by an evil deed" (*Brihad. Up.* IV. 4, 22).

Thus we arrive at some sort of conception, however vague and mystic, of the nature of the Absolute, as held by the sages who wrote the *Upanishads.* When writing on such abstruse and complex subjects one has to be always hedging oneself round from possible misconception and adverse criticism. In so small a book one cannot, of course, make a complete hedge, still one may stop up a gap or two. The *Upanishads* are not inspired, and make no claim to be so; hence they do not move on the same plane as the Bible, though one class of critics may make the claim for them. There is in the *Upanishads* much that is simple, beautiful and true; but, also, much that is artificial, silly and repellent. So, another critic will say, is there in the Talmud with its incredible trivialities, in the spurious Gospels, or in the allegories found in the Epistle of St. Barnabas. Still we find the canonical Scriptures standing apart from all other Scriptures in their grandeur and lofty morality. We do not find in the Bible the Supreme Spirit dividing Himself into male and female. We do not find such false anatomy as a body containing 700 millions of arteries; or an astronomy of a still more childish nature.[1] And as to some of the stories in the *Purânas* one could not translate them without getting into trouble with the police!

[1] What should we think if we found this story either in the Old or New Testament? The gods were one day occupied in churning the ocean to make ambrosia, using Mount Mêru (a mountain many thousand miles high) as their pestle and Âthisêsha (the king of the serpents) as their rope. After swishing their pestle around for some time and producing the ambrosia, the gods stopped to rest, and then Âthisêsha surreptitiously sipped some of the ambrosia and so made himself immortal. The moon which had been looking on told tales of the serpent, and the gods were so angry that one of them took a sword and cut him in two. Âthisêsha could not now, of course, die, and so the head part (Râhu) showed his anger by swallowing the moon; and equally of course, as he could not retain her in his amputated neck, had to disgorge her again. This is the cause of the eclipse of the moon; and to this day every self-respecting Hindu must bathe in the sea, or elsewhere, so as to escape from the poison that falls from the fangs of Râhu whenever he swallows the moon!

CHAPTER III.

CONFLICTING SYSTEMS OF PHILOSOPHY.

THE object of this small book is not to describe all the different philosophic systems which have grown out of the varying conceptions of the Supreme Soul, much less to enter into all the wranglings of those who compete with one another on behalf of their favourite theories, nor yet to discuss the explanations of such modern exponents as the Swâmi Vivêkânanda, who boldly claim that all these antagonistic schemes when rightly viewed mean the same thing. But having sketched the polytheism of the Vêdas, and tried to grasp the nature of the Godhead as expounded in the *Upanishads*, it is necessary to speak, however briefly, of the main systems of philosophy.

These embrace the atheistic dualism of the Sânkhya school, the compromise of the *Bhagavad Gîtâ*, the monism of the Vêdânta as explained by Sankara, and the dualism of the other great *âchâri*, or commentator, Râmânuja.

I. *The Sânkhya Philosophy.*—This need not detain us long because it is a dualistic system completely opposed to the teaching of the *Upanishads* as regards the Absolute One-without-a-second.

Here we have both *purusha*, eternal soul, and *prakriti*, eternal matter. The latter consists of the three "qualities," goodness, passion, and darkness, which by a process of self-evolution produces the world and all that it contains. In this Sânkhya scheme there can be no eternal God and no Creator. We can ourselves easily enter into this philosopher's difficulty. If there be any God, in what way are we to conceive Him? If we say that the Supreme is neutral and unconscious, he argues, how can It create the world? And yet, on the other hand, if this It be conceived as a personal Creator, how can He escape the charge of partiality and cruelty in making some men happy and others miserable? How is the sage to avoid both horns of his dilemma? He does it by practically denying the existence of God, by making matter eternal, and by assuming that individuals rise and fall, and are rewarded or punished according to the principles of transmigration. This latter is the ready means by which so many nations have escaped from their difficulties; but in a later chapter devoted to this subject we shall see that this gap in the hedge conducts us along a path which lands us ultimately into still greater difficulties from which there is no possible escape.

II. *The Bhagavad Gîtâ.*—In this beautiful poem called "The Divine Song," it is generally acknowledged that Hinduism reaches it high-water mark. Bhagavad Gîtâ classes are as popular in the large cities of India as Bible Classes are in those of our own country. The modern educated Hindu, when seriously confronted with Christianity, cries "Back to the Vêdas," he extols the ancient Rishis, chants the Gîtâ, and loudly asserts the orthodoxy of his own particular community. His mind is not disturbed by trifling inconsistencies. It does not trouble him that the Gîtâ supersedes the Vêda, nor that the former is a mere compromise between the orthodoxy of the Sankara school and the atheism of the Sânkhya system. The Gîtâ holds up to contempt "the unlearned men, bereft of wisdom" who prescribed the "flowery doctrine" of the Vêda, and who as "assertors of its exclusive importance" are nothing better than "seekers after their own future gratification". Arjuna is besought (II. 42-46) "to be free from the three qualities" which are the main objects of the Vêdas, and is taught that "as great is the use of a well which is surrounded on all sides by overflowing waters, so great is the use of the Vêdas (i.e. no use) to a Brâhman endowed with true knowledge".[1] We shall also find that the Gîtâ both inculcates a false morality and is tainted with the atheism of the Sânkhya dualism. As every one knows, Krishna, the *avâtar* of Vishnu, appears in the chariot of Arjuna to persuade him that there is no harm in fighting with, and slaying, his own relatives, because in reality there is no such thing as life or death. Every individual soul is the Supreme Soul, and it is only our want of knowledge and the mists of illusion that preclude us from seeing things in their proper light. The following quotation gives the essence of the argument:—

[1] Muir's *Sanskrit Texts*, III. 32.

"Fight, O Bhârata. He who regardeth the dweller in the body as the slayer, and he who thinketh it is slain, both of them are ignorant. It slayeth not, nor is it slain. It is not born, nor doth it die; nor having been, ceaseth it any more to be: unborn, perpetual, eternal and ancient, it is not slain when the body is slaughtered."

One of the chief features of Hinduism is the constantly recurring and marked distinction between the religion or philosophy of India and the emotions and cravings which are to be found deep down in the bottom of every human heart. Divine compassion, divine yearnings and the divine voice which we call conscience, are in the strongest antagonism to the logical conclusions of Hindu speculation and the prescribed observances of religion. We can scarcely help sympathizing with poor Arjuna who is being convinced against his will by the Supreme Deity. If caste duties compel one to stifle these promptings of the heart, there is an end of all moral obligations. As Bishop Caldwell so well puts it, "Krishna's teaching on these heads elevates the conventional duties of the institutions of a dark age above the essential distinction between right and wrong; and we may freely assert that Arjuna's *human*—it may well be styled *humane*—compassion and generosity is far preferable to the strong-hearted philosophy which Krishna professes to be Divine. It is poison administered in honey."[1]

[1] *Krishna and the Bhagavad Gîtâ.*

Still, speaking philosophically, however popular the Divine Song may be among the educated classes of India, it is only a connecting link and a compromise between the atheistic dualism of the Sânkhya system and the theistic monism of Sankhara Âchâri. Moreover, its popularity is largely due to two facts. First, it is a compromise—and we English are no more exempt from a love of compromise than Asiatics—between mystic speculation and polytheism; and, secondly, the Gîtâ makes many concessions to the ancient mythologies, and probably nothing has a greater charm for the child-races of the world—as well as for all actual children—than the romantic stories of mythology.

Before going any further it may be well to sound a note of warning. We all speak, as we are almost obliged to speak, of "Hinduism," the "incarnations" of Vishnu, and of "caste marks". There is no such religion as Hinduism, for there are hundreds of conflicting beliefs; in what we call Hinduism, incarnations are unknown in the ordinary meaning of the word; and caste is never denoted by any marks at all. The marks are sectarian. The followers of the Vishnu sect make a trident, and those of the Siva sect a spot —his third or spiritual eye—on the forehead, but caste is not indicated by any marks and is independent of sect. Language has been cynically defined as the means of concealing thought! Without going so far as this we may note how fatally easy it is to use words in one sense which are used in an entirely different sense by other people, especially by people so widely different from us in every mode of thought as are the people of India. The Hindus, especially the modern graduates of our Universities, are only too fond of asserting that the Incarnation of Christ is the same as that of Krishna, and of invoking the blessing of Brahma—as if it were possible for a neutral, unconscious and impersonal principle to bless anybody. Let the cold-weather visitor to India especially beware!

There is nothing at all corresponding to an incarnation in all the complex warp and woof of Hinduism. There are temporary "descents" (*avatâra*) of the deity upon man and beast, with which Docetism may claim affinity, but no taking of the flesh in any sense whatever. This is the way which Krishna describes himself when he is speaking of the "fools who believe me to be visible":—

"Veiled round about by the mystery of illusion (*mâyâ*), I am not visible at all".

In one passage in explanation of himself he adopts the language of pure monism:—

"I am the father of this world, the mother, the creator, the guardian, the grandsire, the syllable OM, and all knowledge, the Rig, the Sâma and the Yajur-vêda. I am the way, the sustainer, the lord, the witness, the friend, the home, the refuge, the source, the goal, the supporter, the receptacle, and the imperishable seed. I create the heat, I make the rain to cease and cause it to pour down; I am immortality and death, O Arjuna. I am existence and non-existence" (*Bhagavad Gîtâ*, IX. 17-19).

In another passage he declares :—

"I will declare unto thee that which is to be known, the knowledge by which immortality is to be obtained, the highest Brahma without beginning which cannot be said to be existent or non-existent. On all sides it has hands and feet, on all sides heads, faces and eyes, on all sides of the world it has ears, and thus it comprises the whole universe. Beaming in the component element of all senses, it is free from and devoid of all senses. Free from the world it is, it is the support of the universe; free from all the controlling elements (of Prakriti) it uses them" (XIII. 12).

In the first of these passages Krishna declares that he is "existence and non-existence," and in the second he says that "the highest Brahma . . . cannot be said to be existent or non-existent". We have here an admirable illustration of the extreme subtlety of the Hindu mind. First, the Supreme is pure existence and also that in which all potential existence lies, and from which all individuals emanate. Secondly, Brahma cannot be said to be existent, for then It may be looked on as the sum of all individuals and of the material world, instead of a pure intellectual principle; and, on the other hand, It cannot be said to be non-existent, for then there would be the danger of Its existence being denied.

We may accept these seeming contradictions, but when Krishna speaks of himself as being countless faces, eyes, ears, and arms all blazing like a thousand suns, we are outside the region of monism and rather in that of dualism (IX. 16, 17). And yet again, when he says, "Know that Prakriti and Purusha are without beginning; and know also that modifications and qualities are all Prakriti-born," he is evidently trying to conciliate the Sânkhya school, and is in the region of rank atheism. For, as has been shown above, there can be no Brahma, no God, and no Creator where everything is evolved from the three "qualities"—goodness, passion and darkness—which are the constituent elements of Prakriti, i.e. nature, or primordial matter. Thus beautiful as the Gîtâ undoubtedly is, it attempts the impossible when it tries to harmonize the monism of Brahma with the atheism of the Sânkhya dualism.

III. *The Monism of the Vêdânta.*—So much has already been written on monism that one need not dwell long on the Vêdânta, though this is "the end of the Vêdâs"—the essence and kernel of philosophic Hinduism as expounded by the greatest of all commentators, Sankara Âchâri. This philosophy is, of course, based on the Upanishads—the real Bible of the Hindus far more than the four Vêdas to which they are attached, and of infinitely more importance than the epics (the *Mahâbhârata* and the *Râmâyana*) and the idolatrous Purânas—as containing the highest teaching of the Hindu religion. I have already given the definition of Brahma as Existence, Thought and Bliss. There is no real existence except the absolute Self. If we think that a tree is different from a sheep or a man, this is simply due to our want of knowledge and the illusions under which we live. But this explanation seems so absurd that the Vêdântists speak of three sorts of existence: (1) *apparent existence*, e.g. when we see a rope we fancy for a moment that it is a snake; (2) *conventional existence*, such as that of Îsvara, the Lord and Creator of the universe, the Personification of the absolute Self and also of all the creatures whom he has formed; and (3) *the existence of the true Self.* But one of the objects of the Vêdânta is to reconcile differences, and so an explanation has to be found for these anthropomorphic manifestations of the Absolute. Hence we are told that "there are two manifestations of the Brahma, a personal and an impersonal one; the personal one is unreal and the impersonal one is real". Here again the Eastern and Western minds are diametrically opposed to each other. To us it is the personal that is real and the impersonal unreal; to them just the reverse. So too the Vêdântists teach that there are two kinds of knowledge, and in this we can follow them more easily, the subjective knowledge for the initiated, and the objective knowledge for the uninitiated masses. To the former Brahma is always the One-without-a-second. The threefold name Existence-Thought-Bliss is really two-fold, because by Bliss nothing more than absence of pain is meant. But how can the One have two attributes, Existence and Intelligence? The Vêdântist answers that "to exist" and "to think" are really one. When we examine the Christian doctrine of the Trinity in the light of the Incarnation we shall see that this is not so. But to go a step further, when the Vêdântist declares that the Absolute has no self-consciousness, and that when the living soul (*jîva âtmâ*) of man attains to the heavenly Soul (*parama âtmâ*) of the Absolute, it also must lose all self-consciousness; then all "thought" is lost and we arrive at an unreal abstraction beyond the reach of all language and all mental conception. The individual soul can only attain to Thought by becoming no-thought. This looks like intellectual suicide. The Vêdântist, however, sees the difficulty of it as well as we do, and so asserts that the *yogi* by his austerities and abstract meditation attains to absorption into the Self by intuition and introspection.

> "Desirous of immortal bliss, a wise man
> Beholds the inner Self by introspection."

But he is only landing himself thus in further difficulties, for all that appertains to austerities and meditation is itself a product of illusion, and so is unreal; and how can that which is illusive and unreal bring him into real union with the Absolute? No meditation, no intuition, and no introspection can enable him to know the Brahma. It and he are never moving on the same planes, and so by no process of knowledge whatever can he ever attain to the knowledge of the Supreme. The highest virtue of the Christian is love, whereas the highest quality of the Hindu is knowledge (*gnâna*); yet, while for the Christian "love in heaven will shine more bright," the knowledge of the Hindu, just when it is supposed to be bringing him into union with the Supreme, turns out to be the blankest negation of all knowledge.

Since the Vêdântist falls back on introspection for the solution of his problem, we must stop here for a moment to say a word or two on *Yoga*. By severe austerities, by prolonged meditation and by constant practice in the suppression of the breath, the Yogi desires to gain deliverance (*mukti*) from all action and even all thought. For thought and action, whether good or bad, lead to repeated thought and action in other births, and so hinder the final emancipation. The Yogi fixes his eyes on some given object, concentrates —or perhaps one really ought to say abstracts—his mind, and learns to breathe so slowly as almost to cease breathing and to cease thinking. There is no moral end in view, but the persistent practice of such abstraction leads the Yogi at last to exclaim *Brahmâsmi*, "I am Brahma". Now, looked at from our point of view, no austerity can be too severe if it leads to union with the Divine; but, from another point of view, the suppression of the breath must lead to intellectual weakness, as the Hindus themselves well know, for as Barth says of these practices, "Continuously observed they can only issue in folly and idiocy; and it is, in fact, under the image of a fool or an idiot that the wise man is often delineated for us in the *Purânas*".[1] So far then from Yoga helping us to understand how the unconscious Self can be appre-

[1] *The Religions of India*, Barth, p. 83.

hended by our own self on the verge, or attainment, of unconsciousness, it only introduces us to a state of delusion and mental incapacity which is the very opposite of all true knowledge.

IV. *The Dualism of Râmânuja.*—This is the last of the chief systems of philosophy that demand our attention. There are three systems known as monism (*advaita*) One-without-a-second, or modified monism (*visishtâdvaita*), and this last dualism (*dvaita*). At the end of this chapter I shall have something to say of *bhakti*, or devotion to Vishnu, which is the most interesting feature associated with the latter. Râmânuja allows a personal God and a more or less personal existence to the individual. Hence he and the followers of this sect are, of course, in both these respects much nearer to Christians than any other Hindus, and in fact most scholars hold that the Hindus are ploughing with our heifer, since they have borrowed their *bhakti* doctrine direct from Christianity, though there is no direct proof of it. Râmânuja was a commentator who lived and taught at Trichinopoly about the twelfth century of our era ; and we know that from the third century, and probably even earlier, Christians have lived in India. He really believed in three eternal principles: (1) Brahmâ, or Îsvara, the Lord and highest personal Deity—not merely a lower form of Brahma, the impersonal ; (2) the individual soul (*chit*, thought or consciousness), and (3) matter (*achit*, or that which is unconscious). But practically matter does not count when speaking of dualism of this kind, and in this respect differs from the materialism of the Sânkhya system. Râmânuja quotes the following verses to support his dualistic views, and maintains that the "two birds" are not the same, as Sankara would say, but distinctly two—the absolute Self and the human self.

"Two lovely birds, united in close friendship,
  Sit on one tree, embracing one another:
While one of them enjoys the tree's sweet berry,
  The other, looking on, abstains from eating.
The Self on the same tree is sore afflicted,
  And plunged in impotence, with blindness stricken:
If he beholds his mate, the kindly ruler,
  And his great might, he will be free from suffering.
When he, the witness, sees the golden Maker,
  The Self, the Lord, the origin of Brahma,
Then, knowing, he throws off both vice and virtue,
  And, stainless, he obtains supreme perfection."

Dr. Banerjea in his *Dialogues on Hindu Philosophy* makes Râmânuja explain his views about the Supreme Being in the following terms: "All the Sâstras tell us of two principles—knowledge and ignorance, virtue and vice, truth and falsehood. Thus we see pairs everywhere, and God and the human soul are also so. How can they be one? I am sometimes happy, sometimes miserable; He, the Spirit, is always happy. Such is the discrimination. How, then, can two distinct substances be identical? He is an Eternal Light—without anything to obscure it,—pure, the one Superintendent of the world. But the human soul is not so. Thus, a thunderbolt falls on the tree of no-distinction. How canst thou, O slow of thought, say, 'I am He, Who has established the immense sphere of the Universe in its fulness'? Consider thine own capacities with a candid mind. By the mercy of the Most High a little understanding has been committed to thee. It is not for thee, therefore, O perverse one, to say, I am God."

Before closing this chapter it is necessary to speak of the introduction of an entirely new doctrine, namely *bhakti*, because it is the chief element in this system. *Bhakti*, which denotes faith, piety and devotion, arose as a conception entirely new to India. Whether it was derived from Christianity or not cannot certainly be asserted; but if its source was not Christian, then it is difficult to say what it could have been. There is no doubt that Christianity existed in India during the third century of our era, and there is also much internal evidence pointing to a connexion between Christianity and this doctrine, but we cannot safely say more than that. *Bhakti* has nothing whatever to do with the Upanishads and their resultant philosophies; much less does it find a place in the early adoration of the great gods of the Vêdas, or the later idolatrous worship of the three hundred and thirty millions of minor gods in the *Purânas* and modern Hinduism. It dawned on the horizon, we know not when or whence, casting a pale clear light athwart the land, suffusing the hill-tops with a hitherto unseen splendour, while leaving the valleys in shadow. But the face of the earth assumes an entirely different aspect when the first rays of the sun, however faint, begin to lift off the pall of night. Everything is henceforth seen in a truer proportion and with a distinctness impossible during the night, however brightly the stars may shine. And so it was in India. There too the mandate went forth: "Arise, shine; for thy light is come"—at least as a prelude to that fuller command which in later days shall be given, "the glory of the LORD is risen upon thee". When addressing Christians in India we always speak of a devout man as a *bhaktan;* and we expect such an one to display the abiding virtues of faith and goodness, kindness and gentleness. The true *bhaktan*, whether Hindu or Christian, feels a personal attachment and affection which "binds him with gold chains about the feet of God". Everything else sinks into subservience to this attachment. All ritual observances are felt to be void of meaning save as expressions of the heart's union with God. "If he gets this taste, he is filled with joy," declares a Hindu *bhaktan;* and what higher bliss can any Christian aspire to? Later on something will have to be said of caste, the system by which the Brâhmans have crushed and trampled the Pariahs in the mire for centuries, treating them as lower than any dog or pig in the street. Yet what do we read of this new virtue?

"All, down to the despised castes, have a right to it by meditation, as to general truths" (*Sândilya Sûtras*, 78).

Here indeed is a revolution undreamt of before!

Vishnu has always been looked upon as the beneficent God in the Hindu Trimûrtti; and it was in Vaishnavism that the germ of *bhakti* first found its culture and began to develop. So marked is the distinction between this aspect of Vaishnavism and every other form of Hinduism, that Monier Williams declares that "This is the only Hindu system worthy of being called a religion". Now, all this conception is so diametrically opposed to what we have been saying about absorption into Brahma as an impersonal Essence, that one is filled with wonder and amazement, just as a student of physical science would be if he discovered an undoubted case of a biogenesis when dealing with inanimate matter.

It is hoped that the reader will not jump to unjustifiable conclusions and think that every Hindu is a *bhaktan*, and that every *bhaktan* is a Christian at heart. Whether *bhakti* is an importation from Christianity or not, the Hindu's *bhakti* is like a cut flower, beautiful but void of root, or, to change the metaphor, a graceful building, but one without foundation. Apart from the Incarnation, true, living *bhakti* is impossible. When the Hindus have once realized that Jesus Christ is the Tree of life, and the Rock of ages, then indeed, and not till then, will they be able to find a deep root and a sound basis for their devotion, together with the satisfaction of the deepest aspirations of their inmost hearts for union with a personal God.

CHAPTER IV.

THE NATURE OF GOD AND THE TRINITY.

THE Christian reader who has followed the lines of thought in the Vêdas and Upanishads, with the conflicting theories of their different interpreters, will at the same time have been carrying on in his mind a comparison between these ideas and those revealed in the Bible. He will, however, have been in danger of assuming that what he has learnt from his childhood may be taken as a matter of course, and so he may save himself the trouble of thinking things out for himself. He will be apt to take for granted that his own position is impregnable—however imperfect his education in his own religion may have been—and he will also be apt to sit still and listen to others who have thought things out, instead of thinking for himself. In England there is no serious attack of this kind—apart from Hyde Park lectures and infidel literature, which reach a certain class—and therefore there is not much serious defence. Now the missionary's position is different. Whatever he may say will be contradicted by someone. Does he declare, e.g. that all men are sinners and so need a Saviour, his hearer will at once challenge his major premiss and so deny his conclusion. Since the individual soul is one with the Supreme, sin is an impossibility. When, again, he speaks of Jesus Christ as the Incarnate Saviour of the earth, he is at once confronted with Krishna, and told that the two are practically identical; and if he neither knows what is meant by the word *avatâr*, nor clearly understands what is implied by the doctrine of the Incarnation, he will be silenced. If he speaks of the Trinity he will be told of the Trimûrtti (triad) and may soon find himself lost in a discussion on the relative values attached to the immanence and transcendence of God, as held in the Christian and Hindu systems. We have, therefore, to be constantly examining the foundations of our belief, if we are to give any kind of satisfactory answer to the polite, subtle-brained Brahman who is amazed at what he considers our crude, material, and illogical ideas, when the truth spiritual, refined, and logical is staring us in the face. The average blunt, matter-of-fact Englishman is a man of the earth and the plains, while the orthodox Hindu lives on the mountain-tops and breathes an air too rare for the Englishman's lungs.

Now, in the previous pages, the attempt has been made to show briefly, but it is hoped with all truth, what the Hindu's position is—as regards the higher Hinduism—and also to point out the weak places in the fortifications; but that is not enough. We must explain our own position relatively to his. We have seen what a maze of complex and inconsistent ideas is embraced by the word "Hinduism," and we have not yet come to lower Hinduism which is—though in a less philosophical way—just as complex, and we shall find that there is only one key which will fit all the wards of the lock. That key is the Incarnation. By means of this key we shall be able to unlock the secret chamber, to show where the Hindu has gone wrong in his gropings after the truth, and to supply him with that which he needs to make a perfect and complete system, capable not only of solving his intellectual problems, but also—and this is of far greater importance—of satisfying the yearnings of his human heart. But when speaking of the Incarnation we shall first have to prepare the ground by referring to such questions as the nature of God, the doctrine of the Trinity, personality, immanence and transcendence, the nature of sin and its forgiveness, and so on. Here again, only lines of thought will be indicated. These subjects have been treated by many learned theologians, notably by Dr. Illingworth, and the present writer will only venture to follow the guidance of such leaders.

First of all, what is the nature of God? Article I declares that "there is but one living and true God, everlasting, without body, parts, or passions, of infinite power, wisdom and goodness, the Maker and Preserver of all things both visible and invisible". He is life and the source of all life (*vivus* not *vivens*) and so not a bare "existence" (*sat*). He is not subject to transitory passions as we are; He loves because He *is* Love. He is displeased with sin because He is All-holy. He is of infinite power (*immensæ potentiæ*), though His infinity does not preclude the possibility of self-limitation. His wisdom and goodness are similarly infinite. He is Maker of all things, inclusive, of course, of matter; and so cannot be identified with any of the phenomena of the world. He is also the Preserver, the Almighty and All-sovereign, in opposition to the deistic conception which removes Him from all active rule and superintendence over the creatures which He has made. Some deep thinkers, like J. S. Mill, assert that if God is almighty, we cannot account for all the pain, suffering and cruelty in nature, "red in tooth and claw". But does not the Almighty display His infinite goodness in raising mankind, however slowly, from the depths of bestiality and savagery, to which state he has by his sin fallen, into the glorious liberty of sonship with Himself? If we admit the transcendence of the Deity, we are inevitably led on to the idea of personality and Fatherhood. Many Hindus speak of the brotherhood of man which flows from the Fatherhood of God, and many writers seem to claim both ideas as parts of natural religion; but both are purely and distinctively Christian revelations. If we do not accept these statements, then we lapse into Deism, as if GOD were the Divine Clockmaker who had made and wound up His clock, and then left it to go by itself for all time. This view, which was so commonly held about a century ago, even by seemingly orthodox Christians, is now almost outworn, for it is little better than the pagan conception of the gods, who "careless of mankind, lie beside their nectar". Nowadays, men are more apt to conceive of the universe itself as being divine—the clock goes because the works themselves contain, so to speak, the Spirit of the Deity; or else they argue that the universe, from the bare fact of its existence, is divine. Thus we come round from transcendence through immanence to a kind of Pantheism, which is just now very popular among certain classes. This is not, however, as we shall see below, the teaching of the Vêdânta, where GOD is "existence," and all the rest illusory nothingness.

We Christians believe with the Hindu that "GOD is a Spirit"; He is One in three Persons; He is eternal in His *existence*, in His *thought* and in the *bliss* of His divine love; as Spirit He is above all matter and controls all the material universe; He is the Creator of the world by His Will and Word, but is not thereby limited; He is both immanent and transcendent. "In him we live and move and have our being," and yet we do not curtail His majesty, but rather add to His glory by our loyal service; and we hope to attain to union with Him and yet not to lose our individuality or personality. He is our Father and we His children. We also search for knowledge (*gnâna*), but the knowledge that leads up to love—not the supposed knowledge of unconsciousness, or the abstraction of the *yogi*—which is the only complete knowledge; for, "If any man loveth God, the same is known of him" (I Cor. VIII. 3). The correlation of love and knowledge is thus set forth by St. John: "Everyone that loveth is begotten of God, and knoweth God. He that loveth not knoweth not God; for God is love" (1 St. John IV. 7, 8). Again, St. Paul teaches us, with a mysticism and a paradox which remind us of the Hindu sages, that though we only "know in part," yet we are to know the love of Christ which transcends all knowledge, and we are clearly to see the invisible things of God (Rom. I. 20). At the end of a passionate prayer he pleads with the Father for the converts at Ephesus, that they "may be strong to apprehend with all the saints what is the breadth and length and height and depth, and to *know* the love of Christ which *passeth knowledge*" (Eph. III. 19).

We attain to our highest spiritual state on earth when we are carried out of ourselves into the third heaven by an ecstasy of prayer, meditation and communion. We find Him best when we thus lose ourselves. Yet it is not by the abandonment of our own individual gifts, but rather by the highest development of knowledge and love, that we aspire to union with Him.[1] By constant meditation and communion we strive to keep ourselves in God's presence. And in the hope of a more perfect consummation we sing,

> "Till in the ocean of Thy love
> We lose ourselves in heaven above".

The first great difficulty is to treat of the Absolute. Is God One-without-a-second? Does the individual

[1] Cf. "If I lose myself, I save myself," Sir Galahad in the *Holy Grail*.

soul, as a thing apart, trench on His majesty? Does the Supreme lose His infinity in the presence of the finiteness of man? Can the absolute be predicated as both subject and object?

Dr. Illingworth goes into these matters at length, and the following extract will indicate the line of thought:—

"There has always been a double difficulty, one metaphysical, and the other moral, in conceiving the absoluteness of God. A person is primarily and essentially a self-conscious subject; and if we are to think of God as personal, He, too, must be, metaphysically speaking, a subject. But a subject means a subject of experience, one who undergoes experience, or for whom experience exists, and therefore implies as his correlative an object or objects of experience. And the metaphysician is compelled to ask, what can this object be in the case of God? For if we suppose the universe to be this object, we must either regard God as dependent for His realization upon something which is other than Himself; and in that case, His absoluteness vanishes; He ceases to be God: or we must view the universe as a mode of Himself, in a way that leads to pantheism, in which personality is lost. We are driven, therefore, to the conclusion that, if there be any absolute, eternal subject, He must have a correspondingly absolute object, an eternal experience, if His proper absoluteness is to be maintained." [1]

Dr. Illingworth goes on to show that Aristotle held

[1] *The Doctrine of the Trinity*, Dr. Illingworth, p. 136.

that God "cannot be adequately occupied with relative and finite things, and concludes that He must contemplate Himself (νοεῖ ἄρα ἑαυτόν), or, as we should say, be His own object". Now according to the sages of the Upanishads, God can possess no moral attributes. The moral life is a social one. How can God in the solitude of His absolute Nature, apart from His creatures, display the attributes of love, wisdom and justice? And if He cannot, His moral attributes vanish and He ceases to be Divine. Now the doctrine of the Trinity—the Oneness of Father, Son and Holy Ghost—is like a golden key which at once opens the lock. God is love, i.e. He not only has the attribute of love and is the source of love, but *is* in His essential nature *love itself*. He is love, too, from all eternity apart from and before all creation; yet love cannot be love unless it has an object to love. When it is revealed to us that there are the three Persons in the one Godhead, then we understand how the Father loves the Son and the Holy Spirit. He is still the Absolute in contemplation of Himself, as Aristotle says, but He has, also, scope for His love in the threefold personality. So also with the wisdom of God. Wisdom requires an object, for abstract wisdom seems as unthinkable as abstract love. The Son, who expresses and reveals the wisdom of God to man, has, and always had from all eternity, scope for the play of wisdom in the divine Trinity. Then again, as regards the third attribute of happiness in the Hindu conception of "existence, wisdom and bliss," we are not driven to make this quality, as he is, a mere negation of pain, asceticism and so forth, but we assign to it the highest positive value.

When treating of the nature of God we at once get out of our depth, because it has not been revealed to us, and because the finite cannot grasp the infinite. The sages of the *Upanishads* found it easier to speak of the Supreme Soul under negative rather than positive terms: when asked whether Brahma were this or that, they replied *Neti, neti,* not so, not so. And in this way the early Fathers of the Church also wrote :—[1]

"We only reach," says Clement of Alexandria, "in a measure to the conception of God, knowing not what He is, but what He is not" (*Strom.* V. 11). Origen says that GOD'S nature "cannot be grasped or seen by any human understanding, even the purest and brightest" (*De Princ.* 1).

Basil also declares, "That God is, I know; but what His Essence is I hold to be above reason . . . faith is competent to know that God is, not what He is" (*Adv. Eun.* I. 12).

While Gregory of Nyssa writes, "With regard to the Creator of the world, we know that He is, but deny not that we are ignorant of the definition of His Essence" (*Adv. Eun. Orat.* 12).

We may pause here to examine one passage in the Bible which reminds us of the Monism of the Upani-

[1] Quoted by Dr. Illingworth in *The Doctrine of the Trinity*, pp. 103-6.

shads—a passage which has often been interpreted as an attack upon the dualism of the Persians (Aurmazd and Ahriman) as held by Cyrus, and one which has sometimes been seized upon by ill-informed sceptics as if to make God responsible for sin, as is done in the *Mahâbhârata*. In Isaiah XLV. 4-8 we read, "For Jacob my servant's sake, and Israel my chosen, I have called thee by thy name: I have surnamed thee, though thou hast not known me. I am the LORD, and there is none else; beside me there is no God: I will gird thee, though thou hast not known me: that they may know from the rising of the sun, and from the west, that there is none beside me: I am the LORD, and there is none else. I form the light, and create darkness; I make peace, and create evil; I am the LORD, that doeth all these things." At first sight this passage certainly smacks of Orientalism and fatalism. But Deutero-Isaiah would not be likely to attack the religion of Cyrus, who had been appointed as God's instrument for the delivery of the Jews from Babylon. He was rather condemning the polytheism of the Babylonians (Is. XLVI. I), and fostering the monotheism of the Jews. According to the Babylonian myth there was a conflict between Mardük, the god of light, and Timât, the dragon-goddess of the dark depths of the ocean and leader of evil. In opposition to this myth the writer declares that Yahweh is one; He is sole Creator; He is the former of both light and darkness, and the Maker of happiness and misfortune. The Jews had to learn two great lessons

—first, to renounce idolatry and worship one GOD; and, secondly, to recognize the fact that GOD chooses whom He will, like the Gentile Cyrus, to be His instrument, while He Himself remains both sole Creator and sole Ruler of the universe.[1]

The Hindu claims that his conception of the Trimûrtti is in no way inferior to the doctrine of the Trinity; but a brief examination will show that there is no real similarity between the two, and that the Trimûrtti does not help us to solve any of life's enigmas. Just outside the harbour of Bombay lie some small islands, in which will be found a temple cut out of the living rock, and known as the Elephanta Caves. In one of these stands a monolith—a kind of torso—about nine feet high from the head to the waist (*circa* A.D. 1300). The figure has three heads, Brahma in the middle, with Vishnu and Siva at the sides. We are told that these three heads represent God as Creator, Preserver and Destroyer. But Brahma as Creator has entirely dropped out of the Hindu Pantheon, and is never worshipped. Vishnu and Siva in modern times are not only separate deities, each claiming superiority over the other, as the different gods did in the Vêdic period, but are absolutely hostile to one another. In those early days there may have been a trace of the idea of three in one, for the gods were first classified in pairs, Indra-Varuna, Indra-Vishnu, and Soma-Rudra, but later in triple groups such as Agni-Indra-Sûrya as the chief gods. But there is

[1] See the *Century Bible, ad loc.*

another discrepancy. Sûrya is the precursor of Vishnu, but Rudra is not the true precursor of Siva. In the old days Siva was a vile, wicked, and cruel god of the minor class; while in modern times Brahma does not appear at all. Vishnu and Siva now stand alone as the two principal and antagonistic gods. So that we have no Trinity worthy of the name. In the metaphysical conception of the Brahma as given in the *Upanishads*, we find a far closer analogy in the "Existence, Thought and Bliss" to our own conception of the Power, Wisdom and Love of the Triune God. Yet the orthodox Hindu, as we have already seen, does not claim here any idea of threeness, which to him is anathema, but makes the third quality merely a negative term, and declares that the first and second are really the same. The conception of One-without-a-second again blocks the way, and so prevents the Hindu from finding, as we do in the Incarnation of the Second Person, any sort of solution of his difficulties.

And what is the Christian doctrine? "The Catholic Faith is this: That we worship one God in Trinity and Trinity in Unity.

"Neither confounding the Persons: nor dividing the Substance."

I. God *is one.* "Hear, O Israel: the LORD our God is one LORD" (Deut. VI. 4).

II. *There are three Persons in the one Godhead.*

(*a*) "There is one body, and one Spirit, even as also ye were called in one hope of your calling; one LORD, one faith, one baptism, one GOD and Father of all, who is over all, and through all, and in all" (Eph. IV. 4-6).

(*b*) Jesus Christ declared that "Neither doth the Father judge any man, but he hath given all judgment unto the Son; that all may honour the Son, even as they honour the Father" (St. John V. 22, 23). And again, "I live because of the Father" (St. John VI. 57).

(*c*) When speaking of the Holy Ghost he says, "The Spirit of truth . . . shall glorify me: for he shall take of mine, and shall declare it unto you" (St. John XVI. 13, 14).

III. *They are not three* GODS *but one* God.

When our Blessed Saviour was baptized, the Father spoke of the Son, and the Holy Ghost descended like a Dove upon Him. And when He gave His last command on earth He said "Go ye, therefore, and make disciples of all the nations baptizing them into the name (not Names) of the Father, and of the Son and of the Holy Ghost" (St. Matt. XXVIII. 19).

The finite cannot comprehend the Infinite, for the catholic Faith is that we "worship" not "comprehend" such a mystery; yet we may gain some idea of the doctrine of the Trinity in unity by a comparison with ourselves. A man says, "I walk; I think; I pray". It is with the body that he walks, with the mind that he thinks, and with the spirit that he prays, yet there are not three "I's" but one "I".

There is always a danger lest we Christians should become tritheists, believing in the "threeness" of the Godhead, and thus "dividing the substance"; and on the other hand there is the risk of our being deists with the limited conceptions of the Jews and Muhammadans. There is a danger of our also falling into the error of anthropomorphism and forgetting the great truth that "God is a spirit". And we may not only separate the Deity into three Gods, but we, like the Sabellians, may also relapse into the heresy of "confounding the Persons". Reading such a clause as the "Father is over all and through all and in all," we might fancy that we were in the region of semi-pantheism, but are saved from any such misconception by the word "Father"; for the key-note struck is that of a personal God. And so it is from cover to cover of the Bible; wherever we look we find the same evidence of a strong, active, living Personality, the direct antithesis of a neutral, unconscious, and impersonal Essence. God is One and Eternal, the Alpha and the Omega; He is perfect and complete in Himself apart from all individual souls, the Almighty Creator of heaven and earth, and yet not tainted by matter or limited in His Godhead through the existence of the creatures of His own hands. He is absolute Existence, He is Thought, and He is Bliss in no limited or negative sense, but positively and completely as the TRI-UNE. His Name is not an impersonal THAT, but a personal I AM THAT I AM. As Purusha is said to be, He is self-luminous, and He is also the "Light of the world," and the "Father of lights" intellectual and spiritual as well as physical. He is the Father, too, not only of the unique and only begotten Son, but also of all mankind. We declare our belief in His immanence when we say that "In him we live and move and have our being"; and in His transcendence when we say that "God is a spirit"—the Eternal and Absolute, high above all created things and all matter—One God, in direct opposition to the Sânkhya dualistic belief in Purusha and Prakriti, eternal Spirit and eternal matter. The glory of the individual soul is to become "a member of Christ, the child of God and an inheritor of the kingdom of heaven". So far from being absorbed into a kingdom of nothingness, or losing our individual consciousness, we retain to the full our individual personality in the supreme glory of the sonship of GOD.

According to the interpretation of the mystic syllable A U M, as we have seen, the individual passes from the waking stage to something even beyond the state of dreamless sleep. And according to the notion of transmigration, individual souls may pass upwards to the final absorption into the Absolute Brahma, or downwards into the lower births of vegetable or animal life. Now, we Christians divide the world into certain kingdoms, and show how the soul of man may pass into the higher realm. Matter is not eternal, and cannot pass, like Prakriti, into any other stage, or rise into life. Science seems completely to disprove any idea of biogenesis. A blade of grass is higher than a clod of earth, for life of any kind raises the vegetable kingdom above the mineral. Again, the sheep that crops the grass is higher than the grass, because the animal kingdom is superior in many ways to the vegetable. Similarly, the kingdom of man is higher than that of the animal; for man alone can reason and pray. Here we enter into the sphere of personality. But there is a stage still higher, and equally cut off from the lower, unless raised by the miraculous intervention of the Divine agency. "That which is born of the flesh is flesh," and must always remain flesh, unless raised to a higher kingdom by some miracle of GOD. "That which is born of the Spirit is spirit" (St. John III. 6), and those that are thus born in Holy Baptism and led by the Spirit are "children of God" (Rom. VIII. 16). They have been adopted into God's one family, and so have risen to the highest kingdom, and have received the new gift of "eternal life".

In contradistinction to the conceptions of Brahma in the Upanishads let us consider such passages as the following:—

"Giving thanks unto the Father, who made us meet to be partakers of the inheritance of the saints in light: who delivered us out of the power of darkness, and translated us into the kingdom of the Son of his love: in whom we have our redemption, the forgiveness of our sins: who is the image of the invisible God, the first born of all creation . . . and he is before all things and in him all things consist" (Col. I. 12-18).

"The Son . . . who being the effulgence of his glory, and the very image of his substance, and upholding all things by the word of his power, when he had made purification of sins, sat down on the right hand of the Majesty on high" (Heb. I. 3).

"Of him are ye in Christ Jesus, who was made unto us wisdom from God, and righteousness and sanctification and redemption" (1 Cor. I. 30).

In such passages we have practically the four stages in the spiritual life which the Hindu desires so earnestly to develop. He first desiderates *sâlôka*, to dwell in the same world as God, next *sâmîpa*, to be in His Divine Presence, then *sârûpa*, to be in the same image or form, and lastly to attain to *sâyujya*, complete identity with God. The Incarnate Son of God, the Logos—the *chit*, or wisdom of God dwelt bodily (σωματικῶς) on earth (*sâlôka*) among men. After He had taken His glorified body He "went in and went out among" the disciples (*sâmîpa*); He was transfigured before His select Apostles; though "being in the form of God, he emptied himself taking the form of a servant" (Phil. II. 7). So that man created originally in God's own image (Gen. I. 27), and becoming a "co-heir with Christ," dwells in the presence of, and has the same form (*sârûpa*) as, the Incarnate Son. Lastly, he not only gains redemption, justification, sanctification through membership with Christ, and obtains union with Him in the Holy Communion, but hopes also finally to attain to the Beatific Vision when he arrives at the "perfect consummation and bliss, both in body and soul in His eternal and everlasting glory".

Here we have the purest conceptions of both Hindu

and Christian seers. Let us take another passage from revelation: "For this cause I bow my knees unto the Father, from whom every family in heaven and on earth is named, that he would grant you, according to the riches of his glory, that ye may be strengthened with power through his Spirit in the inward man; that Christ may dwell in your hearts through faith; to the end that ye, being rooted and grounded in love, may be strong to apprehend with all the saints what is the breadth and length and height and depth, and to know the love of Christ which passeth knowledge, that ye may be filled unto all the fulness of God" (Eph. III. 14-20).

It may be admitted that when we compare some of the passages in the Upanishads with such a quotation as this, we find that in both there is the same longing for final union with God—though the identity (*sâyujya*) of the Hindu is, of course, different from the sonship of the Christian—the same spiritual tone and horror of materialism, and the same wealth of oriental imagery and rapid transition from figure to figure. But how vigorous, clear, condensed and dogmatic is the Christian teaching compared with the vague, dreamy, negative teaching of the Upanishads. The Apostle bows his knees in humble adoration before the personal Father, with Whom all individuals are associated as in a family. His heart is strengthened by the indwelling, as a welcome guest, of the strong Son of God, through the life-giving power of the Spirit (*διὰ τοῦ Πνεύματος αὐτοῦ*, the *Spiritus*, *Âtmâ*, or *Brahma*). The object in view is that the living soul (*jîva âtmâ*), getting rid of its ignorance (*avidya*), may gain by faith (*bhakti*) the liberation (*mukti*) won by the Saviour, and so attain to the glory of the heavenly soul (*parama âtmâ*). Instead of the human soul losing all consciousness and individual personality, after that knowledge (*gnâna*) has brought it into the Divine Presence, and been swallowed up in It, it is able, as was said above, to apprehend with all other saved souls the breadth and length and height and depth of the love of Christ, which carries it beyond all our limited human comprehension. Instead of the soul being emptied into an ocean of nothingness, it is filled full to the brim from the ocean of the glory of God.

The contrast between the strong and comprehensible Revelation—as far as the finite may be said to comprehend the Infinite—and the vague, contradictory and incomprehensible philosophizing of the commentators on the Upanishads not only shows the impossibility of any true resemblance, but lifts the Christian doctrine as far above all human speculation as heaven is above earth. What Prof. Lebreton says of Greek and Jewish speculations may be made to apply with still greater force to the gropings after the threefold attributes held by the Vêdântists when contrasted with the comparatively clear Christian doctrine of the Triune God.

"Quand, par une laborieuse analyse, nous sommes arrivés à reconstituer les principales théories réligieuses qui pouvaient entrer en contact avec le dogme chrétien de la Trinité, nous constatons entre ces deux ensembles de conceptions un contraste si profond, que nous ne concevons guère la possibilité d'une équivoque et, beaucoup moins encore, d'un compromis. Quel rapport entre le Verbe, Fils de Dieu, et ce logos, force et loi du monde, qui est en chacun de nous germe de vie, principe de pensée et loi morale? Comment confondre le Saint-Esprit, le Paraclet, avec cet air enflammé qui pénétre tous les êtres, qui les enserre, et qui les anime?" [1]

[1] *Les Origines du Dogme de la Trinité* (Beauchesne: Paris).

CHAPTER V.

PERSONALITY.

"The baby new to earth and sky,
  What time his tender palm is prest
  Against the circle of the breast,
Has never thought that 'this is I':

But as he grows he gathers much,
  And learns the use of 'I,' and 'me,'
  And finds 'I am not what I see,
And other than the things I touch'.

So rounds he to a separate mind
  From whence clear memory may begin,
  As thro' the frame that binds him in
His isolation grows defined."

(*In Memoriam.*)

WE have seen that to the metaphysical Hindu personality is an impossibility, whether in man or in GOD. Man cannot be a person, because he is an unreal illusion; and God cannot be personal because as the absolute Brahma, the One-without-a-second, He has no qualities or attributes, no activity or consciousness

—nothing save pure Existence. To the Christian on the other hand personality, both human and divine, is an absolute essential, the starting point in all thought in man, and finds its complete and perfect counterpart in God alone. To those who have experienced it there is perhaps nothing on earth so disconcerting as an earthquake. If we cannot trust the solid earth to keep still under our feet, what is there in heaven or earth or sea that we can rely on? And yet this is but a feeble image to express our thoughts if our personality is denied. If I cannot believe that "I am I," what, then, can I believe? If my personality is an illusion, then everything is an illusion: not only my body and soul, not only heaven and earth, but even the great God Himself is an illusion—everything vanishes and leaves not a wrack behind. My ego, my *jîva âtmâ*, is not only independent of my material body, which it controls, but must be to me the most intensely real thing in existence. If that is not left, nothing is left. The Hindu claims that the existence of the Absolute is left, but on examination Brahma turns out to be an abstract entity, a sublime nothingness, a principle incomprehensible by human thought and unapproachable by human knowledge. If I am not I, then there can be to me no Supreme, because human thought has no basis on which to stand. It is true, as Lotze teaches us, that this living soul, or self, "never rises into complete self-consciousness". Our personality is but a poor, weak thing compared with that of God. "In point of fact, we have little ground for speaking of the personality of finite beings. Perfect personality is in God only, to all finite minds there is allotted but a pale copy thereof."[1]

The orthodox Hindu shrinks from trenching on the majesty of the Infinite by embracing in any degree the finite in that conception; he also has a horror of crude materialism, and so strives, by pushing back thought to its utmost limits, to conceive of the Absolute Self as pure Existence. The Christian, however, declares that man can only conceive of the divine Personality through the analogy of human personality, however imperfect the latter may be. The Hindu does not perceive that by denying the personality of man he is at the same time precluding the possibility of the conception of the Divine—that he is, in fact, cutting the last thread which he has left himself, the thread from which his whole system is suspended, namely, the existence of God.

"The conceptions of divine and human personality vary together. Belief in the personality of man, and belief in the personality of God, stand or fall together. A glance at the history of religion would suggest that these two beliefs are for some reason inseparable. Where faith in the personality of God is weak, or is altogether wanting, as in the case of the pantheistic religions of the East, the perception which men have of their own personality is found to be, in an equal degree, indistinct. The feeling of individuality is dormant. The soul indolently ascribes to

[1] *Microcosmos*, by Lotze, II. 686.

itself a merely phenomenal being. It conceives of itself as appearing for a moment like a wavelet on the ocean, to vanish again in the all-engulfing essence, whence it emerged." [1]

It is almost impossible to define personality and it is difficult to analyse our conceptions of it; and all that can be attempted here is to quote the conclusions arrived at by those best qualified to speak. The fundamental characteristic of personality is self-consciousness. "In all consciousness of self we know ourselves as persons; in all knowledge of other objects we know them as different from ourselves, and ourselves as different from them. Every man is convinced of this; no man can be made to think otherwise. If there be a God, then, as all His works proclaim, He must at least be different from one of His works, He must be different from me. . . . When we restore the conviction of the separate existence of self, and the belief in our continued personality to its proper place, we are removing an effective barrier in the way of the possible introduction of any system in which man can be identified with God, or with anything else." [2]

As Tennyson says, "Is He not all but thou, that hast power to feel 'I am I'?" [3]

All this, of course, is diametrically opposed to the conception of the Hindu sages. Dr. Illingworth tells us that the chief attributes of personality are "in-

[1] *The Ground of theistic and Christian belief*, G. P. Fisher.
[2] *Intuitions of the Mind*, McCosh, p. 453.
[3] *Higher Pantheism.*

dividuality, self-consciousness, self-determination, love and, as the result of their living interaction, character". As regards self-determination, he writes: "The sense of freedom is an immediate part of my consciousness. I cannot be conscious without it. I cannot tear it out. It lies at the very root of myself, and claims, with self-evidence, to be something *sui generis*, something unique." Desire, too, is a co-essential element in our personality. "We require to find in other persons an end in which our entire personality may rest. And this is the relationship of love. Its intensity may admit of degrees, but it is distinguished from all other affections or desires, by being the outcome of our whole personality. It is our very self, and not a department of us, that loves."[1] Thus the constituent elements of personality are reason, will and love, all distinct, yet united in one subject, and developing man's character which represents his whole self.

We cannot fail to recognize the importance of the personal element in our social life. We perceive what mighty forces are at work leading to civilization, human progress, and so on; but at the back of all is seen the person, the leader, the expression of the human will. The teacher may inculcate new and powerful lessons, but it is the personality of the teacher which introduces new life. How much poorer the world would have been, if it had been deprived of the forces brought to bear on it by the personalities of Julius Caesar and Wellington, Pericles and Raphael,

[1] *Personality Human and Divine*, chap. II. *passim*.

Savonarola and Luther, Homer and Shakespeare. And if men with their small intellects and weak spiritual power hold in their hands levers for the movement of the world, what power shall we expect from Jesus Christ, if He be both very God and very Man—the sum of personality both human and divine? That Jesus Christ has so moved the world in a way that no other person has moved it, or could move it, is not only an incontrovertible fact, but also may in itself be an indication of divine Personality. Unless we begin with the assumption that all personality is a delusion, and therefore that God, man, and the universe all amount to zero, then we must recognize the Incarnate Son of God as the divine Lever that moves the world and controls man with all his destinies.

As living beings we think, we will, and we love almost instinctively; and by another instinctive tendency we conceive of God as the only complete and perfect Personality:—

"It is from the intense consciousness of our own real existence as persons that the conception of reality takes its rise in our minds: it is through that consciousness alone that we can raise ourselves to the faintest image of the supreme reality of God. . . . Personality comprises all that we know of that which exists; relation to personality comprises all that we know of that which seems to exist. And when from the little world of man's consciousness and its objects we would lift up our eyes to the inexhaustible universe beyond, and ask to whom all this is related, the highest existence is still the highest personality; and the source of all being reveals himself by His Name I AM."[1]

The higher Hinduism revolves round the word Knowledge, and Christianity treats it as an important factor. Our knowledge of others is extremely limited, yet, as Dr. Illingworth shows, we can only argue by analogy from human to Divine personality. We know a man by our daily intercourse with him. This knowledge is gained only by intimacy. Whether we engage a servant, or appoint an archbishop, personal knowledge is of far greater importance in estimating character—i.e. the sum total of habits which impress their stamp (χαρακτήρ) on the soul—than anything else. No man is a hero to his valet, for the latter knows the hundred and one defects of the popular hero; and familiarity with the petty defects of daily life obscures in his eyes such exceptional events as Trafalgar or Waterloo, or single acts of bravery that may win the Victoria Cross. But again, our knowledge even of our nearest and dearest is at best most imperfect. "Our hermit spirits dwell apart" so that

"Not even the tenderest heart, and next our own,
Knows half the reasons why we smile and sigh".[2]

And if the knowledge of man and wife is so incomplete and limited, how much more must be that of man and God! Yet by analogy only from man can grow our knowledge of God. The humblest farm labourer

[1] Mansel's *Bampton Lectures*, No. III.

[2] *The Christian Year*, 24th Sunday after Trinity.

may, indeed, know God as well as the master of all the sciences—in fact often more easily, because the former has not had his imagination distorted, or his soul materialized by specialization in the secular branches of study. What is chiefly needed to enable us to see God is humility coupled with sincerity. Unless we can put ourselves into the attitude of a little child we cannot enter into the kingdom of God. There must be, however, an earnest and sincere search for God. It was because the Scribes and Pharisees were hypocrites that they were further from that kingdom than the publicans and harlots. One that is harbouring in his heart some secret sin, cannot possibly know God. Only the pure in heart can see God. And why is this? The goodness and purity of God are always blazing forth with a splendour such as the mid-day sun in the tropics, in spite of all the fierceness of its rays, can never rival, and yet the divine Sun shines in vain for one whose optic nerve has (speaking spiritually) been shrivelled, or whose cornea has been destroyed by the violence of deliberate sin, or whose vision has been dimmed by some kind or other of "earthborn cloud". To appreciate Handel, Bach or Wagner one must be a musician, and to enter into the full beauties of Shakespeare or Milton, one must be a poet at heart, though one may never have written eight bars of music or a single stanza of poetry. So as Photinus observes, "He must be godlike who desires to see God".

I have already quoted the remark in *The Hindu*

that "The Hindus have never sunk so low as to believe in a personal God". To do so is assumed to limit the Absolute, to connect the Infinite with the finite creatures of His own hands and to associate Him with the materialism of the earth. Now, the Christian sees no limitation, but rather the expansion of the divine Will, when he says "He spake and it was done". He conceives it no derogation of the divine Majesty to say He "created man in his own image," and made him to be "no longer a bond servant but a son; and if a son, then an heir" (Gal. IV. 7).

The Rishis of the Upanishads started with the assumption that personality is not legitimately predicable of God, and then have been compelled to fall back from one subterfuge to another. But let us see if their assumption is based on fact.

"The common objection—that since personality involves a contrast between an ego and a non-ego, a self and what is outside self, it cannot be predicated of God without implying that He is limited by something which is not Himself—is fully answered by Lotze, who maintains with undoubted truth, that we can clearly distinguish in thought between that immediate state of self-existence which constitutes our ego or self, and the various forms of the non-ego, which are the conditions of its realization; and we can conceive the latter, which do not constitute, but only call out, the attributes of the ego, to be necessary merely on account of our finite nature, and not inseparable from personality as such. . . . The function of the non-ego, in short, our human personality, is not to define its circumference, but to stimulate its activity. And as any possible view of God involves His containing His own principle of activity, He can unquestionably be conceived as personal without any reference beyond Himself."[1]

Again, Îshvara is conceived of by the mystic sage as a Lord for the purposes of creation, but he too, like man, must ultimately fall back into the neutral Brahma at the final consummation. But let us see how far this idea acts upon the practical life of the Hindus. There is now no god in all India so popular as Krishna, one of the *avatârs* of Vishnu. But who is this Krishna that discusses in the divine Song, with his charioteer Arjuna, the mysteries of the Vêdânta, which he endeavours to harmonize? He is surely the strangest medley of character that the world has ever seen. He is not only an *avatâr* of God, and the expounder of the Upanishads, but he is also, as the Hindu books themselves show, the most frankly licentious sinner—thief, drunkard, seducer, and murderer—that history has ever known. And why is he also to the modern Hindu the most popular god in all the Hindu pantheon? It is not in spite of, but in consequence of, his open wickedness; for his very vice demonstrates his intense humanity and makes him so attractive a personality. And this too among a people to whom, speaking metaphysically, personality is an impossi-

[1] See *Microcosmos*, IX, 4, Lotze.

bility! As a matter of fact, the Creator of the world, the Prajâpathi, has implanted in all men's hearts an insatiable craving for personal love. As Mr. Balfour shows in his *Foundations of Belief*, the deepest evidence of all divine teaching is in the intimations and cravings of the ordinary human heart. God has not left Himself without a witness in the world, and, whatever the sages and philosophers may say, the craving of men's hearts must be satisfied—if not in a good way, then in a bad one. Their souls can never be nourished by a neutral, unconscious, impersonal Essence, or any similar abstraction; but they can be fully nourished by a living, loving, and personal Saviour, Son of God. The higher Hinduism is based on Brahma, apprehended by knowledge, but also on Krishna and Râma as its two personal gods; while the lower Hinduism consists in a medley of *karma*, transmigration, idolatry, animism, and devil-propitiation. Christianity is founded on the personality of the Incarnate Son of God; and it is personality that the human heart craves for, with such fervent desire, in spite of all philosophic speculation. Hinduism in none of its phases can *practically* escape from the demands of personality. Krishna and Râma—the two human *avatârs* of Vishnu—as distinguished from those of the boar, fish, lion and tortoise—have touched the heart of all India, because they have struck a chord to which the whole human race must necessarily respond. Man is a social animal, and "it is not good that the man should be alone". Man is also a worshipping animal, and he cannot satisfy the yearnings of his heart apart from personality, even though that personality be as wicked as Krishna, or as hideous and cruel as the goddess Kâli.

Moreover, the mind of man instinctively shrinks from permanent separation from, and loss of friendship and intercourse with, our dear ones beyond the grave —an intercourse infinite in sweetness as it will be endless in duration. We cannot tear them from our hearts: to do so would entail a loss and a grief unfathomable. If bereft of our individual personality, we should not only lose ourselves, but we should lose those whom we love more deeply than ourselves, and, above all, lose the communion with the Most High, a joy that passes all human understanding. The words of the philosopher-poet leap to our lips :—

> "That each, who seems a separate whole,
> Should move his rounds, and fusing all
> The skirts of self again, should fall
> Remerging in the general Soul,
>
> Is faith as vague as all unsweet:
> Eternal form shall still divide
> The eternal soul from all beside;
> And I shall know him when we meet:
>
> And we shall sit at endless feast,
> Enjoying each the other's good:
> What vaster dream can hit the mood
> Of Love on earth? He seeks at least

Upon the last and sharpest height,
Before the spirits fade away,
Some landing-place, to clasp and say,
'Farewell! We lose ourselves in light.'"

(*In Memoriam*, XLVII.)

The fact that all the races of the earth have a belief of some sort in God can, after recent research, scarcely be called in question; though it may, indeed, be admitted that some religions are not worthy of the name religion. Still this fact seems to confirm the idea of a personal God. Daily we hear of some new theory which threatens the belief in God and boasts that it will upset all historic religions; but the world wags on as before, the ephemeral theory finds an early grave, and is forgotten in the next fanciful conceit, which will in turn have its little day and die. Nietzsche, for instance, assures us that the great principle of the world is "Will to power"; that life is strife; and that there is nothing so immoral as morality, or nothing so vicious as mercy, goodness and selflessness —those very qualities that the two hundred million Hindus admire most of all, to say nothing of all Christendom. There is nothing new in such a selfish grasping for power at the point of the bayonet, any more than there is in the thousand and one other suggestions of Satan under the guise of philanthropy which are always cropping up. Through them all stands out the one great fact that "The LORD our God, the Almighty, reigneth," as the one Supreme

Ruler of the universe; and, also, the other fact that the great mass of the nations of the earth believe in Him, in however distorted a form, not excluding the bulk of the Hindus as well.

The chief virtue of the Christian believer and one of the constituent elements of his personality, is love; but the chief desideratum of the Hindu, as we have already seen, is knowledge (*gnâna*), and it is by knowledge only as the fruit of meditation, austerities and the practice of *yoga*, that the Hindu gains the perception of the fact that he himself is the Supreme; that his individual ego is identical with the Absolute Ego; that his own soul is one with the eternal Brahma; and it is then that he exclaims in the words of "the great sentence" of Hindu theology, *Brahmâsmi*, "I am Brahma". Now the Christian also needs knowledge, though knowledge does not occupy, as with the Hindu, the primary position. Knowledge leads to love, and love connotes personality. "This is life eternal, that they should know thee the only true God, and him whom thou didst send, even Jesus Christ" (St. John XVII. 3). It is only by knowing God that he can love God; he cannot possibly *love* any abstraction however sublime. And to know God he must first be known by Him. "Knowledge puffeth up, but love edifieth. If any man thinketh that he knoweth anything, he knoweth not yet as he ought to know; but if any man loveth God, the same is known of him" (1 Cor. VIII. 1-4). And St. Paul looks forward to the time of complete knowledge: "Then shall I know fully even as also I have been known fully" (ἐπιγνώσομαι καθὼς καὶ ἐπεγνώσθην, 1 Cor. XIII. 12). But knowledge is only a means to an end —the apprehension of the Christian's "great sentence," God is Love. Yet, strange to say, the Brâhman who lifts knowledge up to the highest pedestal, gains nothing by his knowledge, for, before attaining absorption into the Deity, he himself must have passed to a state even beyond the reach of dreamless sleep. Then again, conversely, love leads on to yet fuller knowledge. "I pray," says St. Paul, "that your love may ever grow and grow, in the attainment of perfect knowledge and universal discernment."[1]

And not only is it impossible for man to love any save a personal God, but it is also both impossible to sin against Him, or to meditate on Him. The Hindu admits the former on the ground that he is himself essentially divine, and the Divine cannot sin. The Christian rather argues that if God is an abstraction, sin is impossible, for we cannot offend, or transgress the laws of "That"—an unconscious, neutral and impersonal principle. So too as regards meditation. How can the *yogi* gain the supreme knowledge 'Thou art That'—that Brahma—by his meditation on what is as unthinkable as the flame of a candle when blown out?

Now, no one can deny that the Hindus have occupied the first place in the history of the world in "feeling after God if haply they might find Him". Nor has that search been trivial or half-hearted, much less arro-

[1] *Paraphrase of Philippians*, I. 9, by Bishop Lightfoot.

gant or supercilious. A life of seclusion, wholly cut off from the pleasures of the world, and accompanied by hunger and nakedness, by weary pilgrimages, and the austerities of *yoga*, by torture and self-mutilation —all these have they gladly endured in the quest for God. It is true that in India religion and morality are divorced, and the sternest ascetic sees no more harm in breaking half the Decalogue than we do in killing a mosquito—which to him is indeed sin—still, one often finds the temptations of the flesh sternly resisted in the longing to find the Right Way. I was particularly struck with this when reading the Tamil poems of Tâyumânavar.[1] He describes with evident pain the struggle he had to endure, after making his renunciation, when he looked into the bright laughing eyes of those who had before enslaved him; and goes on with the deepest pathos to lay bare his longing for God, and his desire to attain to a state of absolute quiescence, when every movement of the body, every uttered word, every innermost thought of the mind shall have died out in the approach to Brahma. A few stanzas are here translated to illustrate this frame of mind; and the personal touch of one living in comparatively modern times adds to the interest:—

"O Supreme Deity, my miserable mind brooding again and again over unthinkable thoughts has become wounded.

O Supreme Deity, seeing that my mind is filled

[1] This poet lived in Trichinopoly nearly three centuries ago. His name means "Both father and mother," and is a synonym for God.

with deceit and lying, I clamour with envy. Can there be any Right Way for such a soul as mine?

O Supreme Deity, night and day it is my great desire that words and their meanings should cease, and that I should become absolutely quiescent.

O Supreme Deity, can there be any deliverance from births for me, unless speech dies out and I become as silent as a dumb man, and so become one with Thee?

O Supreme Deity, my Father, the complete renunciation of the mental faculties is the highest renunciation of all."

(*Parâbhara Kanni.*)

When reading such pathetic lines as these, the same feeling comes over us as when we see some blind man stumbling about and groping his way over a broken road. We long to take him by the hand and guide him, or, better still, to perform some operation by means of which we may restore him to sight. He has renounced, as far as he can, the world, the flesh and the devil; he desires to give up, also, the gifts of the senses and all else that makes life worth living, if only he may attain to union with the Supreme. Are not we English Christians, who reject his religious tenets, put to shame by his utter self-sacrifice? It is his own religious guides who have destroyed his sight, and so rendered him incapable of beholding the God for Whom he longs. For such as these the Incarnate Son of God stretched out His arms on the Cross when drawing all men to Himself.

It is Jesus Christ, then, as a divine Person, Who can alone satisfy men's needs. "Before Abraham was I AM," says the eternal Son. "He is the image of the invisible GOD, the firstborn of all creation," says St. Paul (Col. I. 15). He is Man above all men. He spake as never man spake, and with an authority that awed His hearers. He consulted no man, for He knew what was in man; and when the impulsive Peter placed himself on the same level as his Master —"Be it far from thee, Lord: this shall never be unto thee"—he was rebuked in the sternest language. Yet, what man was ever more human than the Son of man, "Who became flesh and dwelt among us," Who "wept with those that wept, and rejoiced with those who rejoiced"? As perfect Man He summed up all mankind, all the "living souls" of the Upanishads: and since He "died for all, all died," or, rather, "all were dead" (*ἀπέθανον*, 2 Cor. V. 14). Again, by "becoming obedient unto death" (Phil. II. 8), He both carried out the will of a loving Father, and constituted Himself the Saviour of the world. And as He stretched out His arms to all mankind, however perverse, so is the devout Hindu now in turn stretching out his groping arms to Him as a still unknown Saviour.

CHAPTER VI.

IMMANENCE, TRANSCENDENCE, AND PANTHEISM.

BEFORE proceeding any further we must plunge into a somewhat abstruse subject, namely the immanence and transcendence of GOD. English theologians have lately given a good deal of consideration to these matters, and it will be clear from what has already been said that Hinduism contains much that bears on the same. That Hinduism is pantheistic seems generally to be taken for granted, but it is very doubtful if this view is correct. If philosophers define Pantheism in terms of the teaching of the Vêdânta, then, of course, Hinduism is Pantheistic; but if we accept as a broad definition the common phrase, "God is everything, and everything is God," then certainly Hinduism is not Pantheistic. As we go on we shall find that the doctors differ very considerably, both as regards the immanence of God, and the existence of Pantheism in Hinduism. But I think that we shall also find that all these riddles, like so many others, can be solved by the Incarnation of Jesus Christ, and by that alone.

Bishop Mylne (formerly of Bombay) writes: "The Hinduism of which I shall treat is not that degraded idolatry which prevails in the India of to-day. Its thirty-three millions of divinities [this is a slip of the pen for three hundred and thirty millions] are but concrete embodiments and expressions of the single pervading belief that God is all that exists, and that everything that exists is divine. For Hinduism, in its every stage, is at bottom really pantheistic. . . . In each of its stages, I say, the core of the religion was the same—GOD is everything and everything is God."[1] And the Bishop holds that this is so not only in the "purely and professedly Pantheistic stage of the Vêdântic books," but during the "nakedly and unblushingly polytheistic stage of the Purânic literature". As most people assume that at least the Vêdânta is Pantheistic, this view must be examined with respect, but it cannot be allowed to pass unchallenged. One or two general remarks may be made in passing.

If I were asked, I should say that sacrifice, not pantheism, is the core of the Vêdas; that transcendentalism, or a mystic philosophizing leading to agnosticism, is the substance of the Vêdânta; that *karma* and transmigration, with the worship of Vishnu and Siva, tinged with the Vêdânta, are the chief features of the modern Hinduism of the higher castes; and that idolatry, sacrifices, animistic cults, devil-dancing and so forth are the characteristics of the Hinduism of the lower castes and out-castes. I should also deny that "everything that exists is divine". From the Vêdântic point of view nothing, apart from Brahma,

[1] *Mankind and the Church*, p. 310.

exists, and "everything" is a mere illusion. Looking at it from the point of view of lower Hinduism, one tree is sacred and another is not; while one animal is god, another is vile and unclean. So that we can scarcely say that "everything is God".

For the present we will see what is to be said of immanence and transcendence in Hinduism from the point of view of writers such as Bishop Mylne. According to this view Vêdântism is the extreme expression of the immanence of God. The Bishop expresses well the relation of the Absolute Brahma to man when he says: "Either the finite is included in the Infinite—has no existence apart from it—and then you have no finite—or else it is excluded from the Infinite—and then you have no Infinite; it is limited by the very exclusion" (p. 339). A philosophy which only recognizes spirit lands us in "the thorough-going pantheism of the Hindu," while that which only recognizes matter forces us into "the thorough-going materialism of a Haeckel". If the finite has no existence apart from the Infinite, then the Creator does not differ from the creature, the Worshipped from the worshipper, the Giver from the gifts, the Thinker from the thought, or the Potter from the pot. To quote a favourite simile of the Bishop—"Man is but the ripple on the stream, the ripple rises and is again lost to rise again in a thousand little wavelets, while the stream flows on irrespective of its varying modes which are but parts of itself".

Again, he says that the Hindu's "Pantheistic conception of God is but the thought of His immanence run mad," and the difference between the Hindu and the ordinary Christian is this: "A Hindu's thought about God in His relations with nature and with man are exclusively concerned with His immanence; whereas in English popular theology His transcendence is alone kept in mind" (p. 332). In the latter part of this sentence there is only too much truth. The blunt, common-sense Englishman has a horror of anything like mysticism, and so he tends to become a crude materialist—the *bête noire* of the Hindu. The Hindu charges the Christian with a belief rather in Law and a mechanical universe instead of a God immanent in all creation; while the Christian retorts that the Hindu's logic forces him into the belief that God is responsible for all the wickedness in the world. This latter is a point that needs brief expansion. The Brahman is strictly, nay inexorably, logical; but see where his logic leads him! The shameless licentiousness of the god Krishna, the unspeakable barbarities of the goddess Kâli, and the innumerable wickednesses of men, what are these, and whence do they come? They are inevitably the expression of the One-without-a-second. In God there is no good, no bad; no love, no hatred; no purity, no lust; no kindness, no cruelty; no holiness, no wickedness. They are all simply modes, or expressions, of the Supreme; they are all mere ripples on the stream. The Hindu conception, then, breaks down because it ignores—and must ignore in its irresistible logic—the spiritual sense. But the spiritual sense cannot be stifled; it is stronger than any logic and overleaps all barriers. The conscience, which God has implanted in every human heart as the witness of Himself, refuses to be silenced. We are, therefore, bound to reject the philosophy of the Vêdânta, however logical and complete, because our moral sense revolts against an acquiescence in immorality.

Now, let us look at our own position, with which most of us Christians are satisfied. We believe in the absolute transcendence of God; and that there is a great gulf fixed between the Spirit which created the world and the world which He created. But the Hindu will turn round upon us, and we must answer, if we can, his questions. Do you not believe in the immanence of God? Can you conceive of a Creator distinct from the creature, or of the finite apart from the Infinite? How can there be a Father and a Son, so far distinct as is implied in the usual meaning of these two words? Do you believe that the Spirit created the world, and then left it as a stone to roll down the hill? You reject with us the materialistic view that matter is independent of Spirit, but are you not practically theists? By ignoring the immanence of God you make the world move on mechanically and independently of the Creator. Ought your God to be called God at all? Would He not more correctly be described as Law? The average uninstructed Christian can give no reply to these questions. Why? Because he has never thought out for himself, or never been taught by others what is meant by the Incarnation of the Son of God, however glibly he may talk about it. What, then, shall we say? We believe both in the transcendence and immanence of God. "In him we live and move and have our being." God not only created the world as the Logos, "through whom all things were made," but sustains the world, for "in him all things subsist". As Bishop Mylne maintains, the transcendence of God must be tempered by His immanence. If the Logos is Incarnate, then the immanence of God in His creation is a necessity. The Word was made Flesh, and became "the Man"; He abode, while in the flesh, in the world of His creation; and He effected its redemption, so that in the beautiful words of St. Athanasius, "God became human that man might become divine". Arguing from the Pantheistic point of view the Bishop shows that immanence alone lands us in the immoral conclusion that God is responsible for all the evil in the world; while transcendence alone lands us in materialism and a negation of a divine Ruler of the world. Combine the two through the Incarnation and the gulf is spanned. Think of God through the Logos as not only creating the world, but as ever sustaining all creation; think of Him not only as very God but as very Man—not "a man," but as "Man," Who has taken all humanity into Himself—and the whole difficulty disappears.

Dr. Illingworth teaches us in his *Divine Immanence* that we must study human personality, as it is only by analogy from ourselves that we can gain any conception of the Divine. Our spirits are immanent in our bodies. The expression of our faces, the touch of our hands and the tone of our voices are the reflection of our inmost feelings. But the spirit is also transcendent over the body; for we possess qualities that rise above matter, though they express themselves in the material world. In our individual personalities we are, then, both immanent and transcendent. If we admit the force of this contention, we shall see how natural it is to accept the Incarnation as the connecting link which binds together both the immanence and transcendence of God in His relation to man.

But are the Father and the Son distinct? As God is *ex hypothesi* perfect and complete, how can that completeness be predicated before the Incarnation when the Son took humanity into Himself? We have already seen that the Triune God comprises Power, Wisdom, and Love. God is love; and God must not only be love but must have an object of love. God is not only Thought but the Word, the expression of thought. In the blessed Trinity the three Personalities existed and loved, were perfect and complete before the creation. We see the "immanence of the creature in the Deity, Who called it from nothingness" when the due time had come. So the Incarnation "anticipates the kindred problem of the immanence of God in creation when once He has called it into being". The Hindu believes that God repeatedly descends for a time upon some one of His creatures for some specific purpose, and this He does owing to His immanence in creation. But the Christian believes that the Incarnation could never be repeated. "It means that once in the fulness of time, a Person of the Triune GOD, Who not only is immanent in all things, but Who infinitely transcends them all, took into His own divine Being the spiritual and bodily essentials of a perfect human nature."[1]

There is much that is true in what Bishop Mylne says, and much that is both forceful and beautiful in this line of argument, but, starting with the same premiss as to the relation of the absolute Self to the individual self, we are brought to a very different conclusion. There is nothing *real* in the whole universe, nothing save the One-without-a-second; all else is *mâyâ*. But what is this *mâyâ*, or illusion? Whenever a Hindu is in difficulties he falls back on *mâyâ;* but what is it, and where does it lead us? Since nothing exists save Brahma, *mâyâ* does not exist. Yet it is due to *mâyâ* that we imagine that the universe exists. Thus we know that the universe is unreal, and yet the *mâyâ* itself which is responsible for our false conception is also unreal, for it is an illusion of human consciousness, and the human being who is supposed to be conscious is himself all an illusion. This reminds us of the old difficulty of our schoolboy days—"All Cretans are liars," but supposing the person who makes this statement is himself a Cretan, what then? So, according to this method of reasoning, it is obvious that there can be no Pantheism in the Vêdânta—the very

[1] *Mankind and the Church*, p. 374.

thing on which Bishop Mylne so strongly insists—and if there is none in the Vêdânta there is certainly none elsewhere in Hinduism. Colonel Jacob in his *Manual of Hindu Pantheism* (p. 15) expresses much surprise that "the great reformer Râmmohan Roy saw in them (i.e. in the Upanishads) nothing but *monotheism*". A modern missionary writing from Benares expresses himself very emphatically on the subject in *The East and The West*:—[1]

"To say that the monistic Vêdântism taught by Sankharâchârya (and this appears to be the most consistent and clearly-thought-out form of Vêdântism) is in any sense allied to Pantheism is to contradict the very clearest teachings of the system. The essential characteristic of Pantheism is to maintain the immanence of God in the universe; in fact, to maintain that the universe is God and to deny His transcendence. The essence of Vêdântism is, on the contrary, to maintain His transcendence, and to deny His immanence. The position of the Pantheist is that all that is—meaning by that the whole material universe and all that comes within the scope of human knowledge and experience—is God, and there is no Being above and distinct from this All. The Vêdântist's position is far removed from this. He does not say that 'All is God,' but that 'God is all,' which is a very different position. His meaning is that *God alone is*, and that of nothing else can it be asserted that it *is*. The All of the Pantheist does not exist for the Vêdântist at all; it simply

[1] *Is Hinduism Pantheistic?* by the Rev. E. Greaves, April, 1911.

does not really exist; such as it is, it is the product of *mâyâ*; it is an illusion of human consciousness, and the consciousness itself—nay the very human being who is conscious—are both alike merely illusive existences. The universe which is conceived, and the mind which conceives it, humanity, and the gods are all no more real than a dream. They are a dream, and the dreamer himself is likewise but a dream. In some way or other beings which do not have any real being imagine that they exist, and imagine themselves to be in a universe which is not, and to pass through experiences which have no real occurrence. Nothing really exists but God. He is not a Person; He (or It) is devoid of consciousness, of emotion, and of volition; He neither thinks nor acts. The rendering which is sometimes given of a Sanskrit phrase, 'There is one God, there is no other,' is utterly misleading. This rendering would lead one to suppose that the phrase taught pure monotheism, but this is not the case. The right rendering is, 'There is one (thing), namely, Brahma; there is nothing else'. This teaches that there is only one thing that really exists, namely, Brahma (God); everything else which we regard as existing does not really exist at all. Thus God is not immanent in the universe, for the universe does not exist; He cannot create a universe, for He is so utterly *Oneness* and *Sameness* that there is no possibility of the slightest movement within His being which will result in consciousness or thought, far less such movement as is necessitated by the idea of creation. This extremely rigid monism is as utterly opposed to the essential elements of Pantheism as anything well could be. It is quite time that the current charge about Hinduism being Pantheistic should be withdrawn."

It will be well to stop for a moment to consider the use of such words as "God," Creator," "Incarnation," and "Pantheism". We English people are so accustomed to use words in our own sense—e.g. speaking of "God" and connoting the idea of personality therewith—and to fit them to alien ideas, because we find them ready to hand in our vocabulary, that we attribute to others tenets which they would repudiate for themselves. The orthodox Hindu speaks of the Brahma as the Self, but does not think of Him as "God" in our personal sense. To him Brahma is not a "creator," for it is inconceivable that an unconscious Essence could create anything; though Brahma may be said to have created the illusion known as the universe. Again, there is no real "Incarnation," since none of the "descents" of Vishnu are of the same kind as the "becoming Flesh" on the part of Jesus Christ. Lastly, there is no Pantheism in our ordinary sense of "God is everything, and everything is God".

Going back to our two authorities is there any possible reconciliation of their antipodal views? According to the Bishop, the "Pantheistic conception of God is but the thought of His immanence run mad" According to the other writer immanence is impossible. and it is transcendence that has run mad; also, monistic Vêdântism is in no sense allied to Pantheism.

Which of the two is right? This is what Colonel Jacob says in his commentary on the Vêdântasâra (p. 49):—

"The characteristics of Brahma have already been considered in the opening notes, and it is in accordance with the doctrine of existences, as there explained, that Brahma is here declared to be the only reality (*vastu*). All else is unreal (*avastu*), and imagined by ignorance. This is plainly put in the *Adhyâtma-Râmâyana* (*Yuddhakânda*, VI. 49, 50): 'The entire universe, movable and immovable, comprising bodies, intellects, and the organs, everything that is seen or heard, from Brahmâ down to a tuft of grass, is that which is called Matter (*prakriti*), is that which is known as Illusion'."

Thus we have two things which are really only one thing. There is, first, the neuter Brahma, which is the only reality; then, secondly, there is the masculine Brahmâ and everything else below him, which is *mâyâ*, that is nothing at all.

According to the same authority (p. 47), Ignorance (*ajnâna*) is synonymous with nescience (*avidyâ*) and illusion (*mâyâ*) and "though called the material cause of the universe, nevertheless heads the list of unrealities!" . . . "It is *not describable as existent or non-existent*." If allowed to have true existence, dualism of course ensues; and if it be said to be non-existent, it falls into the same category as a hare's horn, the son of a barren woman, and such-like absolute nonentities, and no causation could then be attributed to it. So to avoid the dilemma, it is said to be neither the one nor the other. Howbeit, it is acknowledged to have a practical existence, and to have been eternally associated with Brahma; and as a matter of fact, Brahma and Mâyâ are the exact counterpart of the Purusha and Prakriti of the Sânkhya, which is a professedly dualistic system.

So practically we have not to deal with one "existence" but two. First, there is the "existence" known to the sage, who has withdrawn from the world, and who strives by the attainment of knowledge to gain release from the fetters of worldly existence. To him there is only one true "existence," namely that of the self-existent Brahma. Everything else that *seems* to exist apart from Brahma is nothing more than an obscuration of Brahma due to mâyâ. Secondly, there is the "existence" of other Hindus living the ordinary life of the world. According to their unenlightened minds there is a kind of existence, caused by this obscuration of Brahma, which is practically a reality for ordinary people. The phenomena of the world "from Brahmâ down to a tuft of grass" do not exist in the highest sense of the word, but do exist in the sense that for our finite minds they *appear* to exist.

This, of course, does not reconcile our difficulties, but it helps us to look at matters from two entirely opposite points of view. Beginning with Brahma plus mâyâ we find Brahmâ and all the phenomena of the world. All these apparent existences may be said to be embraced in Brahmâ as the Îsvara, the Lord or

God. And so the Hindus may speak of "God" as omniscient, for all finite intelligences are included in Him. He is, also, omnipotent, in the sense that all finite powers are embraced by Him; He is also a Creator, in the sense that all the world is included in Him. Similarly, we may argue that Hinduism is pantheistic. The transcendent Brahma is declared to be "beyond the range of speech or thought," and Brahmâ is the highest association of Brahma with mâyâ. Hence it may be argued that Brahmâ, as God in the Hindu sense, is the sum total of all finite existences, and therefore that Hinduism is pantheistic. We may follow the orthodox Hindu in his subtle argument, but the fact remains, as Mr. Greaves has shown, that the Vêdântist's position is not that "All is God," but that "God is all," in the sense that "*God alone is*, and that of nothing else can it be asserted that it *is*". Though we deny that it *is*, we may admit that it *appears;* but is this Pantheism? Pantheism has been defined as a theory of the universe which identifies God with the sum of finite existences. Now in the Vêdânta God is nowhere identified with the sum of finite existences. There are *really* no existences, save the One Self-existent. Another definition given is that God is a single Principle of which all the phenomena of the world are manifestations. If Pan theism means that God is the sole reality, while the phenomena of the world are mere appearances without any independent existence, then we may admit that Hinduism is in this limited sense pantheistic. But in the generally accepted sense that "Everything is God, and God is everything," Hinduism is certainly not pantheistic.

It may, indeed, be argued that the Bhagavad Gîtâ is pantheistic in tone; but in so far as it teaches that the phenomenal world has some reality, however shadowy, it teaches dualism, and not the monism of the Vêdânta. Some remarks by Bishop Caldwell on this head are worth quoting :—

"According to the Gîtâ, God is the soul of the world; its material cause as well as its efficient cause. The world is His body, framed by Himself out of Himself . . . . The most wicked actions which men, vainly fancying themselves free agents, are ever tempted to perform, are not only permitted by God, but are actually perpetrated by Him, inasmuch as they are performed by His power and will, working out their ends through the human constitution, which is a part of Himself. This doctrine differs, it is true, from the Advaita doctrine, to which alone the name of Vêdântism is popularly given, that the Supreme Spirit alone really exists and that the world is unreal; but it may be regarded as questionable whether the unreality of phenomena be not preferable to the doctrine that their reality consists in their inclusion in God as parts of His totality."

Going back to the subject of immanence and transcendence, Bishop Mylne declares that the Hindu's "Pantheistic conception of God is but the thought of His immanence run mad". The opposite view is that the teaching of the Vêdânta is not immanence but transcendentalism of the most extreme kind.

Mr. Greaves declares that, "The essential characteristic of Pantheism is to maintain the immanence of God in the universe; in fact, to maintain that the universe is God, and to deny His transcendence. The essence of Vêdântism is, on the contrary, to maintain His transcendence, and to deny His immanence."[1]

Here, again, we have two antipodal views. According to one immanence has run mad in Vêdântism, and transcendence been utterly ignored; according to the other immanence is impossible, and it is transcendence that has run riot. Now, whichever of these views we adopt—and to my own mind the latter seems unanswerable—it is clear that *both* immanence and transcendence are essential to a right conception of the relation of God and man. Immanence alone, unlimited and logical, as the Bishop proves, will drive us on to depths of vice, and drag even the Deity down into the same mire. The fatal flaw in Pantheism is that it must include in God the wickedness of men. Transcendence, which ignores immanence, rises to such heights of transcendentalism that it carries us into an atmosphere too attenuated for mortal lungs to breathe. In the presence of such extremes rational argument seems impossible. So, as a matter of fact, whether Hinduism hangs on immanence or transcendence, its position is indefensible; whereas according to the

[1] "Is Hinduism pantheistic?" *The East and The West*, April, 1911.

doctrine of the Incarnation of Jesus Christ we have the two coupled together, as Bishop Mylne shows, by a golden bridge. Jesus Christ, the God-Man, is immanent in all creation, and yet transcendent in that He is superior to all creation. Not only is it in Him that "we live and move and have our being," but He is "the first-born of all creation" (Col. I. 15). He is the divine Personality, the representative of all mankind, and the totality in which all men are embraced. He is, also, through the Holy Ghost, the Parama Âtmâ Who acts upon and controls all the material universe, and pervades the life of all mankind. Yet, though He unites in His Person both immanence and transcendence, there is no dualism, much less that materialism from which all true Christians shrink as instinctively as do Hindus. As we say in the *Quicunque vult*:—

"Although He be God and Man, yet He is not two,
but one Christ;
One; not by conversion of the Godhead into flesh,
but by taking of the Manhood into God;
One altogether; not by confusion of Substance, but
by unity of Person".

If the line of argument thus indicated is sound, then we are not only able to solve the riddle that seemed inexplicable, but we also see how strong and impregnable is the foundation of the Christian belief compared with the speculations of Hindu philosophy. The Christian Church is not built on a quicksand, but on the Rock of ages. We have had the advantage of the full light of revelation, whereas the Hindus have only had a few twinkling stars to help them in their search for the unknown God. Yet how earnestly have they sought for Him! How terribly they put us careless, worldly-minded, money-seeking Christians to shame, in their rejection of materialism and in their struggle to attain to the loftiest pinnacles of the spiritual life. Clement of Alexandria said: "Perchance philosophy was given to the Greeks, directly and primarily, till the LORD should call the Gentiles" (*Strom.* I. 5). May we not apply the same beautiful remark to the Hindus? The LORD is now calling the Hindus, and some day they will add their contribution to the common store—it may be of subtle penetration into the divine mysteries, or the method of mystic communion with the Most High—but whatever it may be that contribution will not be the least valuable addition to the treasure-house of Christendom.

CHAPTER VII.

SIN AND ITS FORGIVENESS.

WHEN we trace the conception of sin in Hinduism from the earliest ages to the present time, we find that the whole idea changes as we pass from the polytheism of the Vêdas (1500-1000 B.C.) to the sacrificial period of the Brâhmanas (from the sixth century B.C.), from the metaphysical ideas of the Upanishads and the Bhagavad Gîtâ down to the idolatries and other gross practices as witnessed in the common life of the great bulk of the people to-day. Though the latter constitute the lower form of modern Hinduism, and will be referred to in the last chapter, we must not fall into the error of considering them as necessarily the latest product of Hinduism, because they are probably the modified survivals of religious observances which date back to a period long antecedent to the Âryan invasion. But viewing the whole course of Hinduism, and speaking generally, two facts seem to stand out prominently. Whether we look at sin in New Testament language as a snare and stumbling-block (*σκάνδαλον*), a missing of a mark (*ἁμαρτία*), a falling away from the right path (*παράπτωμα*), or as a spirit of disloyalty and lawless transgression (*ἀνομία*), we find nothing in

Hinduism which *adequately* expresses the heinousness of sin and the separation from God. Secondly from the point of view of an abstract Essence, unconditional and void of attributes (*nirguna*), sin is manifestly impossible. We *cannot* sin against an abstract principle, and can only sin against a God that is personal. And now let us take a bird's-eye view of the Hindu conception of evil. In the Vêdas we find the idea thus expressed:—[1]

> " Free us from sins committed by our fathers,
> From those wherein we have ourselves offended.
>
> . . . .
>
> Not our own will betrayed us, but seduction,
> Thoughtlessness, Varuna, wine, dice, or anger.
> The old is near to lead astray the younger:
> Even sleep removeth not all evil doing."
>
> (*Rig Vêda*, VII. 86, 5, 6.)

Here there is at least a conception of sin, though there is no deep appreciation of its vileness. Again,

> " If one should flee afar beyond heaven,
> King Varuna would still be round about him ".
>
> (*Athara Vêda*, IV. 16, 4.)

There is no escape from Varuna's vengeance. Another poet in another land expressed it so in similar strain:

> " If I ascend up into heaven, thou art there:
> If I make my bed in Sheol, thou art there ".
>
> (Psalm CXXXIX. 8.)

[1] Cf. Dilger's *Salvation*, p. 292.

Varuna is the upholder of law and order, and so the chief references to sin are found in connexion with him.

> "His nooses stand spread out to catch the man that tells a lie."
>
> (*Rig Vêda*, IV. 16, 6.)

Yet he is also a tempter to sin and with the other gods sets traps for wrongdoers.

> "May he protect us from Varuna's temptation, from the temptation of the great God."
>
> (*Rig Vêda*, I. 128, 7.)

To conceive of God as capable of tempting man to sin shows the lowest conception of the nature of Him Who, if God at all, must *ex hypothesi* be All-holy. And although sin is often spoken of in the Vêdas as an "offence," a "trap" (σκάνδαλον), an "injury," and an "act of thoughtlessness," it never seems to be looked upon as a breach of loyalty to the Supreme LORD, an act of disobedience to the Heavenly Father, or a wound to the heart of the King of Love. The prevailing idea is the escape from punishment, and the Âryan never rises to the height of the Christian poet who sings:—

> "Be of sin the double cure,
> Cleanse me from its guilt and power".

The Hindu's aspiration is to be relieved from a double burden—the penalty of guilt and the treadmill of existence—but he knows nothing of this "double cure". Nothing corresponding with the 51st Psalm can be found in the whole range of Hindu literature. The Hindu rishi looks round in perplexity and cries:—

> "Neither the right nor the left do I distinguish,
> May I attain the broad light free from peril".
> (*Rig Vêda*, II. 27.)

But here, again, he does not pray with the confidence of another Christian poet:—

> "Lead kindly light, amid the encircling gloom,
>
> . . . .
>
> Keep Thou my feet; I do not ask to see
> The distant scene; one step enough for me".

In a hymn addressed to the Fire-god, Agni, occurs the refrain,

> "May his light chase our sin away".

This is probably a prayer that the sacrificial flame will purify the soul, and so induce God to deal more leniently with the sacrificer. Still, sin was a reality to the Åryan; it was felt to be a burden, and the whole land was deluged with sacrificial blood. The word "sacrifice" occurs more frequently in Sanskrit than in the Hebrew of the Old Testament. But as time went on, the sense of sin grew more dim and the ritual of sacrifice more meaningless. The chief object of a sacrifice was not a vicarious one, but a means of gaining power even over the gods. The two evils against which Gautama waged most persistent war were barren sacrifices and caste; and he succeeded far more with the former than the latter. As also the idea of Brahma developed, the conception of sacrifice naturally began to die; for, as said above, man cannot sin against an abstraction. The sacrifice also became more and more of an impossibility as the notion of metempsychosis took root. If our ancestors have passed into animal forms, all animals must be protected as sacred; for to tread on an insect, or to catch a fish, might be to commit one of the most serious crimes possible against one's nearest relative or dearest friend. But the process was gradual in growth.

Passing from the Vêdas to the Vêdânta let us see what the teaching of the latter is about the doctrine of sin:—

"By no deed soever is his future bliss harmed, not by theft, not by a Brâhman's murder, nor by a mother's murder, nor by a father's murder; nor, if he wishes to commit sin, departs the bloom from his face" (*Kaushîtaki Upan.*, III. 1).

"The thought afflicts him not, 'What good have I left undone, what evil done?'" (*Taittirîya Upan.*, II. 9).

"Evil adheres not to an enlightened man, any more than water clings to a leaf; but much sin sticks to the unenlightened man, just as lac to wood" (*Mahâbhârata*, XII. 299, 7).

Well may Dr. Banerjea say, "Vêdântic authors have boldly asserted that they are subjected to no law, no rule, and that there is no such thing as virtue or vice, injunction or prohibition".[1]

[1] *Dialogues on Hindu Philosophy*, p. 381, quoted by Col. Jacob in *Hindu Pantheism*, p. 128.

Men have always been troubled, as the illiterate coolie of to-day is, with the questions, "If God is good, why did He allow sin to enter into the world?" and, "What is the origin of evil?" The early sages did not wish to charge God with the creation and introduction of sin into the world, and so they tried to show that man is responsible for his own deeds whether good or bad. In the Divine Song Arjuna asks:—

"What is it, O Varshneya, which drives man, even against his will, to commit sin?" and Krishna answers:—

"It is lust, the force which springs from passion; it is the will. Learn to know this wasting, all-devouring foe. It is an unquenchable fire. The senses, emotions and intellect are its kingdom. It clouds the free perceptions of the soul and darkens the recognition of the truth" (*Bhagavad Gîtâ*, chap. III.).

Still, this is not pure monism: the Divine Song is only a compromise. According to the pantheistic theory that men are manifestations of Brahma, then Brahma is, in the last resort, just as responsible for the bad as for the good. The following quotation reveals a transitional state in which both Brahma and man are responsible for sin:—

"That Self is indeed Brahma, consisting of knowledge, mind, life, sight, hearing, earth, water, wind, ether, light and no-light, desire and no-desire, anger and no-anger, right or wrong, and all things. Now, as man is like this or that, according as he acts and according as he behaves, so will he be: a man of good acts will become good, a man of bad acts bad. He becomes pure by pure deeds, bad by bad deeds. And here they say that a person consists of desires. And as is his desire, so is his will; and as is his will, so is his deed; and whatever deeds he does, so he will reap" (*Brihadâr Up.*, IV. 4, 5).

As we go further on we arrive at absolute monism, the Self is everything, both good and bad, man is not responsible; Krishna, the drunkard and adulterer, becomes the favourite god; and sin, as we understand it, is an impossibility. As already shown (at the end of chapter II.) such thoughts as "I have committed sin, I have done good" can never rise to the mind, because the Brahma is above all such conceptions.

We saw that the ancient sages shrank from the horrid blasphemy of making God responsible for man's sin. The *Mahâbhârata*, however, does not hesitate for a moment to throw the responsibility of sin on Brahmâ, as the Creator of the world:—

"It is not right, O prince, that the penalty of what is the doing of one agent should be paid by another. 'Let it fall upon Him'—with these words put it down to the Creator, from whom it issues" (*Mahâbhârata*, XII. 32, 16). Beginning with the assumption of the One-without-a-second, and passing on to the conception of Brahmâ, as the Lord, irresistible logic drives one to the conclusion of associating God with sin. One would think that such a startling conclusion would force men to investigate their premisses once more. But no; the orthodox Hindu has another method. He escapes quite easily from all the difficulties consequent on such a conclusion, for as the commentator Sankara shows, all such ideas are merely the products of *avidya*. It is only our lack of intelligence that makes us imagine there is such a thing as sin. The whole thing is an illusion, the mirage of the desert. In recent years the Swâmi (lord) Vivêkânanda has lectured to audiences (ever craving for some new thing) in America and England, and one of his favourite declarations is that, "men can commit no greater sin than think that they are sinners". Granted that there is no personal God, the conclusion is, of course, obvious. We cannot offend an Essence. The orthodox Brahman will, indeed, admit a kind of defilement. He may be, and in fact is, contaminated as he passes through the round of 8,400,000 existences, but such contamination does not touch his essential nature. He will explain his views by this illustration: Take the case of muddy water, the mud has got nothing to do with the water. You see water one day as steam, another day as ice, another as the sap of a tree, or the juice of the fruit that you eat. Condense it, melt it, filter it, distil it, and you will get the original pure essence, water. If man is essentially God, then sin as we understand it is impossible; and therefore, of course, no Saviour is necessary. Colonel Jacob admirably sums up the teaching of the Vêdânta on this subject:—

"The line of argument adopted by . . . the apologists is unsafe, and does not get rid of the fact that some of the Upanishads, the chief source of the Vêdânta doctrine, do, *without any qualification*, declare that sin and virtue are alike to one who knows Brahma; and the system is therefore rightly charged with immorality. But, independently of such teaching as this, what moral results could possibly be expected from a system so devoid of motives for a life of true purity? The Supreme Being, Brahma, is a cold Impersonality, out of relation with the world, unconscious of Its own existence and of ours, and devoid of all attributes and qualities. The so-called personal God, the first manifestation of the Impersonal, turns out on examination to be a myth; there is no God apart from ourselves, no Creator, no Holy Being, no Father, no Judge—no one, in a word, to adore, to love, or to fear. And as for ourselves, we are only unreal actors on the semblance of a stage!"[1]

The Drâvidian races still sacrifice (as we shall see in the last chapter) thousands of kids, buffaloes, and even unclean pigs; and we shall find in these sacrifices a striking resemblance both to the totem observances common to the whole uncivilized world, and also to our own Holy Communion. There is the blood bond, the shedding of blood on the ground to appease the wrath of the Deity and so to atone for sin, the eating together of the sacrificial victim, and so on. All this is necessarily opposed in every way to the teaching of the

[1] *Hindu Pantheism*, p. 129.

Upanishads, but the modern Drâvidian considers himself an orthodox Hindu for all that.

In the face of such conflicting views the ordinary arguments on the Atonement, with which we Christians are familiar, do not seem to apply. The missionary must first try to find some *ποῦ στῶ*. When dealing with an orthodox Brâhman there is the usual difficulty of monism round which every problem revolves. When the hearer is, however, a staunch believer in transmigration, one can try to rouse the conscience with the words of the *Mahâbhârata*, "It is not right that the penalty of one man's action should be paid by another". When the belief in sacrifices is maintained the task becomes still easier. One can show that sin is lawlessness in its widest sense (*ἡ ἁμαρτία ἐστὶν ἡ ἀνομία*, I St. John III. 4). The whole world is under the law of order, and transgression of law brings its own penalty with it. A man who leaps from a housetop breaks his leg; one who eats bad or poisonous food becomes ill or dies; one who is guilty of theft or murder is imprisoned or hanged—the instrument here is a person, not a law or a disease; while one who commits adultery suffers from the remorse of conscience, which tells him that he has caused grievous offence, and one can only offend a Person. The evidence of many Hindu sages also corroborates the voice within. The sacrifice which has almost lost its meaning in the mists of empty ritual and senseless observances, is felt to be full of life and force when applied to the Incarnate Son of the living God.

But forgiveness is not an easy matter, as Archbishop Magee proved. We need not put our hands into the fire, but we cannot escape the penalty if we do. God will not interfere to prevent the pain. We need not eat poison, but if we do we shall die. We need not commit murder, but if we do, the judge, however merciful and kind, will condemn us to be hanged. So, if we commit adultery, though we may escape the secular arm of the law, we shall for ever suffer the torture of remorse, where the "worm shall not die, and the fire shall not be quenched" (Is. LXVI. 24). How, then, is it possible to escape punishment? Humanly speaking, it is impossible. Nothing but a miracle can save us. The "glad news" is that "Jesus Christ is the propitiation for our sins" (1 St. John II. 2). He has acted in some way—we know not how—by means of which it has been possible for God to intervene between the transgression of law and the penalty which automatically follows from that transgression. A stone must fall to the ground when thrown up, and a man in the sea must be drowned. But St. Peter was enabled to hold the law of gravitation in abeyance just as much as his Divine Master, and just as long as his faith in that Master held firm. The basis of the Atonement is not knowledge, but love. The Father does not demand from the Son a cruel death as a bargain—"a wicked God trying to save a wicked man in a wicked way"—as the Archbishop put it; but the Son Himself gave His life as a willing sacrifice, and as the highest act of a Personal Saviour. "God so loved the world that he gave his only begotten Son, that whosoever believeth on him should not perish, but have eternal life" (St. John III. 16).

Dr. Chatterji, of Bengal, said at the Edinburgh Missionary Conference that the great stumbling-block in the way of his own conversion rose from the difficulty of believing that one man's death could remove another man's guilt. This is one of the commonest objections that daily confronts the evangelistic preacher in India. The Incarnation, rightly viewed, solves the problem. It is not a case of pitting one man against another. Sin is not a normal act, but an abnormal state, just as sickness is something alien to the normally healthy body. Man's soul is in a state of disorder and must be set in order. Jesus Christ by His Incarnation took all manhood into Himself that He might bring the world back to its normal condition; and He has removed the obstacle from our path, so that it is now possible, as said above, for God to intervene between the violation of law and the punishment that should be the consequence of that violation. In other words, forgiveness, though it demanded no less a penalty than the death of the Son of God, is now possible. This is the doctrine of the Atonement, not of the Incarnation, but apart from the latter the former would be inexplicable.

The mystery of the Incarnation and the Atonement is, of course, beyond our finite comprehension, for—to adopt a pregnant phrase of Mr. Balfour's—"Unless it was too vast for our intellectual comprehension, it would surely be too narrow for our spiritual needs".[1] When Krishna is explaining his presence on earth he says: "Whenever, O Bhârata, good custom languishes, and evil custom increases, I create myself. For the protection of the good, for the destruction of evil-doers, and for the restoration of good custom I am born in every age" (*Bhagavad Gîtâ*, IV. 7, 8). The Incarnation of our Blessed Lord means far more than this. It not only led on to a vicarious sacrifice on His part, such as the Hindus have never known, but leads on our part to the justification, sanctification, reconciliation, and final glory of man. "While we were enemies, we were reconciled to God through the death of his Son" (Rom. V. 10). Also, when writing to the Corinthians, St. Paul says, "But ye were washed, but ye were sanctified, but ye were justified in the name of the Lord Jesus Christ, and in the Spirit of our God" (1 Cor. VI. 11). And again, to the Romans, "If Christ is in you, the body is dead because of sin; but the spirit is life because of righteousness. . . . As many as are led by the Spirit of GOD, these are sons of God. . . . Ye received the spirit of adoption, whereby we cry, 'Abba, Father'. The Spirit himself beareth witness with our spirit, that we are the children of God; and if children, then heirs; heirs of God, and joint-heirs with Christ; if so be that we suffer with him that we may be also glorified with him" (Rom. VIII. 10-18).

The Hindu believes either that he is incapable of

[1] *Foundations of Belief*, by A. J. Balfour, p. 259.

sin, or, feeling the pricks of conscience, strives to pacify his goddess by slaying a kid, making a weary pilgrimage to bathe in some sacred stream, offering a coco-nut to the idol in his temple, or employing a devil-dancer to gyrate round a fire to propitiate some vindictive spirit or blood-thirsty demon; but he knows of no definite method of gaining forgiveness, and never dreams that he must make his own life correspond in some measure with the nature of an all-holy God. Religious he is, and often eager to spend his days in fastings and his nights in austerities, but he sees no necessity for being moral. Religion and morality have no necessary connexion in his mind.[1] With the Christian the two things are bound together inseparably. The true follower of Jesus Christ sets daily before his mind, as his aim, that "sanctification without which no man shall see the LORD" (Heb. XII. 14); and, as his standard, nothing lower than perfection—to be perfect even as his heavenly Father is perfect (St. Matt. V. 48).

[1] One of the eighteen recognized forms of charity is to give a *sannyâsi*, or ascetic, money to satisfy his animal passions.

CHAPTER VIII.

KARMA AND TRANSMIGRATION.

THERE are here two conceptions different in age and origin, but united in Hinduism in such a way as now to be inseparable. They will be treated in order, and then viewed from the standpoint of the Incarnation.

We have already seen that in accordance with the Upanishads a Hindu cannot sin, yet every devout Brâhman is supposed to repeat daily in Sanskrit his confession of sin: *pâpobam, pâpakarmâham, pâpâtmâ, pâpasambhavah*, which literally means, "I am sin, I commit sin, my soul is sin, and I am conceived in sin". We found that in the Vêdic period the sense of sin was a reality, and streams of sacrificial blood had to be shed to expiate it. Manu, in his Laws, gives a classification of sins with a suitable list of tortures in the next life and penances in this. We have also seen that all India abounds with sacred places and cleansing streams for the washing away of sin. But besides all these, *karma*, with the kindred idea of transmigration—which are, as they have been for a score of centuries, the two most widely pervading ideas throughout India—are doctrines based on sin. Most people are aware that this word *karma* denotes that action springs from action, and results in further action in endless succession.[1] The idea, like so many others in Hinduism, is, of course, unthinkable; for the human mind demands that a chain of cause and effect must begin somewhere and end somewhere. The will is supposed to energize into action, and each action becomes the cause of some other effect, and so cause and effect revolve for ever and ever in endless sequence like the wheels of some tireless engine constructed on the principle of perpetual motion. This ruthless Juggernaut crushes out all ideas of justice and mercy; and as the results of good actions are thrown off with machine-like precision in the shape of rewards, so the penalties of evil actions are ground out in the shape of inexorable retribution. *Karma* is, in its Hindu conception, a blind, mechanical, cruel, remorseless system; and no one—not even the gods themselves—can put a spoke in these wheels. At the back of all lies *Adrishta*, an "unseen," but irresistible influence. There is no room here for the existence of a personal God, for a redeeming Cross, or for a Throne of grace.

At the bottom of the doctrine we find the pessimistic notion of the evil of existence. Where there is no strong grasp of the idea of personal existence in eternal joy there can be only one possible answer to the

[1] The reader must be careful to pronounce the short "a" like "u" in "curd". If he pronounces it long (kârma), as was done by one of the speakers at the Edinburgh Missionary Conference, he may be thought to refer to Kâma, the goddess of lust.

question "Is life worth living?" But what must one do to get rid of the burden of existence? With a possibility of 8,400,000 re-births staring one in the face, and each existence carrying with it a vast predominance of misery over joy, the desire "to cut short the 84 lakhs" is not a thing to be wondered at. How is this to be done? By curtailing action. The great question of life is not "What shall I do to be saved?" but, "What must I do to escape *samsâra?*" (earthly existence).[1]

The doctrine of *karma* seems traceable to two sources, the Sânkhya philosophy and Buddhism. The latter, as we know, though driven out by Brâhmanism, produced the most profound modifications in the whole trend of its rival's system. According to the Sânkhya philosophy, as we have already seen, everything is produced by *Prakriti*, primordial matter, and this is composed of three *gunas*, or qualities. These *gunas* are goodness (*sattva*), passion (*rajas*) and darkness (*tamas*). Now, this matter with Purusha (Spirit) are "both without beginning"; hence we have the atheistical conception of eternal matter as the basis of the universe. Moreover, Krishna in the Bhagavad Gîtâ

[1] As Monier Williams well says: "Transmigration is the great bugbear, the terrible nightmare and daymare of Indian philosophers and metaphysicians. All their efforts are directed to getting rid of this oppressive scare. The question is not, What is truth? Nor is it the soul's desire to be released from the burden of sin. The one engrossing problem is, How is a man to break this iron chain of repeated existences? How is he to shake off all personality?" Cf. also Slater's *Higher Hinduism*, pp. 191, 206-7.

declares that "all qualities whether good or bad" proceed from himself, and that goodness, passion and darkness are all from him and in him (VII. 12).

Krishna thus defines *karma:* "The expansion that causes the birth of beings is called *karma*" (VIII. 3). And beings are compounded of these desires and passions which in turn are always generating new actions, and so must be destroyed before the soul can be free. So, Krishna says in another place, "He whose intellect is everywhere unattached, the self-subdued, dead to desires, he goeth to supreme perfection from *karma* by renunciation" (XVIII. 49). According to their theory there is no God, the soul is passive and eternal matter reigns supreme.

Now, how did Gautama look upon these things? The GOD of the Brâhmans was to him an object of terror; the soul, as he found, could not be cured of its arrogance and selfishness by any asceticism; and existence was a state of misery. So he began by denying GOD, then he next repudiated the existence of the soul—which put an end to all idea of the transmigration of *souls* as far as Buddhism is concerned—and, lastly, arrived at the conclusion that nothing survives save the effect of actions. The fruit of actions can never die, but must for ever reappear till all desires have been starved out, all thirst for existence quenched, and the blissful repose of Nirvâna attained. Thus Buddhism teaches transmigration of *karma*, but not that of the soul. So from these devious sources flows the idea of *karma*, a mechanical principle, higher than God; eternal in its working out of cause and effect, and inflexible in its exaction of the uttermost farthing as the penalty of sin. *Karma* makes Nature supreme, and Nature is always cruel and relentless—fiercer than the tiger's claw, and sharper than the serpent's tooth.

And now let us turn to the second idea of transmigration, which has been wedded by the Hindus to *karma* so as to become one doctrine.

If one were to ask what is the central feature of modern Hinduism as held by the upper and middle classes, in distinction from the idolatrous practices of the lower classes, one would assuredly answer that *karma* and transmigration affect the minds and lives of the majority of the people more than anything else. In discussing the matter with the Hindu, in spite of the fact that transmigration is like a nightmare crushing the life out of the soul of the people, one finds, of course, that he considers his own religion to be complete, self-contained, and far superior to every other religion that is, or has ever been, known in this world. Yet his own Vêdas and the histories of many other religions, are all against him. There is no trace of transmigration in the first three Vêdas, and it is only when we come to the fourth (the Yajur Vêda) that we find any reference to the new teaching.

In fact the first Vêda is distinctly opposed to it. The departing soul is thus apostrophized as it departs:—

"Go forth, go forth on those ancient paths on which our forefathers departed. Thou shalt see the two kings delighting in Svadhâ (libation), Yaêma and the god Varuna.

"Come together with the Fathers, and with Yama in the highest heaven, as the fulfilment of all desires. Having left all sin, go home again, and radiant in thy body, come together with them" (*Rig Vêda*, X. 14, 7).

It may be of interest to note here in passing a remark of Yama's to show how different were the ancient and mediaeval views on this subject of death. When Prajâpathi obtained immortality by his sacrifices, Yama indignantly exclaimed, "If all men become immortal, what portion will remain for me?" Transmigration was during that period a thing unheard of.

When the modern Hindu begins to read Shakespeare he is surprised to find the doctrine there, and that too attributed not to the Hindus but to the Greeks.

> "Thou almost makest me waver in my faith
> To hold opinion with Pythagoras,
> That souls of animals infuse themselves
> Into the trunks of men."
>
> (*Merchant of Venice*, IV. I.)

When he is told that Pythagoras (about 604-520 B.C.) very likely borrowed his ideas from the ancient Egyptians, he is still more incredulous. According to Herodotus there is no doubt that the Egyptians held this doctrine, and it is highly probable that Pythagoras learnt his theories when residing in their country. It is a far cry from Pythagoras to Mrs. Besant, but both these exponents profess, what every believer in it surely ought to be able to do, namely to remember the actions of their previous existences. Pythagoras was, in the earliest birth which he remembered, a son of Hermes; then he fought in the Trojan war; and in a still later existence recognized the shield of Menelaus, by whom he had been wounded in that encounter. So far from the old Âryans having evolved the conception, or having had it revealed to them by their sages, it is not at all improbable that they gained the idea from the aborigines of India, as the Romans did from the Druids of ancient Britain, with whom, as the poet Lucan tells us, death was not the *janua vitae*, but the middle of a prolonged life.[1] Pythagoras gives a space of a thousand years' punishment before a re-birth occurs, and surmounts the memory difficulty by asserting that the disembodied spirits have to cross the plain of Lethe and drink from the river, the remembrance of the past in the following existence being in inverse proportion to the copiousness of the draught drunk. In one respect Plato resembles the Hindus, and that is in his love for astronomical periods of time. Nothing less than ten thousand years will satisfy him as to the period between death and the return to the former state, because it takes all that time for the disembodied one to grow his wings again, and so follow the god in his flight! The Hindus differ from Pythagoras in the fact that they do not fix the exact

[1] Regit idem spiritus artus
Orbe alio: longae (canitis si cognita) vitae
Mors media est.

period of purification, or the exact number of souls that are always going through their re-births; though both theories land one in practical difficulties, especially the latter, as soon as one begins to reflect on the smallness of the world's population in the prehistoric ages compared with the ever-increasing number of individual souls which every fresh census of the world's population reveals. There can be little doubt that the Jews were also troubled with the idea of God's partiality and even cruelty, as the Sânkhya philosophers express it, when they recognized the fact that some men are born into the world blind; and no solution of the difficulty ever seems to have presented itself to them apart from the sin of the parents, or that of the child, in some previous existence (St. John IX. 2). We need not spend time in speaking of Cæsar's reference to the subject in the *De Bello Gallico*, or of other Latin poets;[1] but we can scarcely pass over the exquisite lines of our modern poet Wordsworth who in his *Intimations of Immortality* seems to carry us, whether intentionally or not, into the region of metempsychosis.[2]

"Our birth is but a sleep and a forgetting:
The soul that rises with us, our life's star
Hath had elsewhere its setting,
And cometh from afar:

[1] Omnes una manet nox,
Et calcanda semel via leti.
(*Horace*, I. 28, 15.)

[2] The Alexandrine Father Origen was a believer in a modified form of re-incarnation.

Not in entire forgetfulness,
And not in utter nakedness,
But trailing clouds of glory do we come
From God, Who is our home."

Much less need we waste our time in considering the modern craze for a *réchauffé* of transmigration fancies, as there are always a number of idle busybodies, wearied with the *ennui* of a barren life, who love to fashion eclectic phantasies of their own, imagining that they have discovered some startling novelty.

The doctrine of transmigration seems to have taken root in India somewhere between 1000 and 700 B.C. It was certainly in vogue when Buddhism was becoming a power in the land in the sixth century; and Gautama himself had at one time been "a monkey on a river bank," and in another birth "a virtuous elephant". It became incorporated with *karma* as a necessary consequence of that belief and is found full-blown when the Divine Song and the Laws of Manu were written. The basis of the idea is the evil of existence, a burden which must somehow or other be got rid of. All matter is essentially evil. Man is made up of the three *gunas*, goodness, passion and darkness, and though different people possess these qualities of goodness and badness in varying proportions, they cannot get rid of actions, and actions flow on for ever by the law of *karma;* and as the bodies die the souls go on ever performing their weary Sisyphean toil, entering new bodies of men, Brâhmans or Pariahs, animals or worms, trees or stones, with intervals of purgation where they "eat up the fruits of their former merits or demerits".

It may be of interest here to give a quotation showing the process by which souls pass step by step along "the Path of the Fathers":—

"But they who conquer the worlds (future states) by means of sacrifice, charity, and austerity, go to smoke, from smoke to night, from night to the half month of the decreasing moon, from the half month of the decreasing moon to the six months when the sun goes southward, from these months to the world of the fathers, from the world of the fathers to the moon. Having reached the moon, they become food, and then the gods feed on them there, as King Soma is fed upon with the words "increase and decrease". But when this (the result of their good works on earth) ceases for them, they return to ether, from ether to air, from air to rain, from rain to earth. And when they have reached the earth, they become food. They are offered again in the altar-fire of woman. Thus they rise upwards to the worlds and go the same round as before. But those who know neither of these two paths become insects, birds, and all sorts of biting vermin" (*Brihadâr Upanishad*, VI. 1, 19).

Though transmigration both among the Hindus and Greeks is the result of *sin*, under the influence of the passion and darkness derived from Prakriti, or of the Furies according to Greek mythology; yet we must not forget that in Hinduism good actions as well as bad lead to re-incarnation, and so retard that deliverance (*mukti*) which only can be obtained by the utter loss of thought and consciousness. Moreover, the body is not only an evil thing to be got rid of, but it has no more to do with our souls than have our clothes, which we change as we please.

"As a man casting off worn-out garments taketh new ones, so the dweller in the body, casting off worn-out bodies, entereth into others that are new" (*Bhagavad Gîtâ*, II. 22).

The fact, so simple and obvious to us Christians, that the body is sacred, is part of our true selves, and is as much a gift of the good God as the mind and the soul, never seems to have impressed itself upon any of the Oriental sages; and because of this defect all manner of impossible theories had to be invented.

A full refutation of the doctrines of *karma* and transmigration does not fall within the scope of this essay, for we are dealing primarily with the Incarnation of Jesus Christ; and so only lines of thought which that dogma covers need be indicated.

It is quite clear that we Christians hold a doctrine of *karma*, for such passages as the following at once suggest themselves:—

"Thou renderest to every man according to his work" (Ps. LXII. 12).

"Whatsoever a man soweth, that shall he also reap" (Gal. VI. 7).

"For we must all be made manifest before the judgment-seat of Christ; that each one may receive the things done in (or through) the body, according to what he hath done, whether it be good or bad" (2 Cor. V. 10).

Again, we cannot be saved except by a process of re-birth. "That which is born of the flesh is flesh," and never can become anything else except by the miraculous intervention of God's Holy Spirit, any more than a stone can become a plant, or a horse can become a man. "That which is born of the Spirit is spirit," and hence in Holy Baptism we are regenerated and made "new creatures" (St. John III. 5; 2 Cor. V. 17). St. Paul, also, gives the comfortable assurance that "Sin shall not have dominion over you; for ye are not under the law, but under grace" (Rom. VI. 14). Hence our evil actions cannot always be rising up against us, and degrading us from our noble state as sons of God to the level of the brute creation. Union in the Nature of the One God makes man a joint-heir with Christ and a son of God—a person dwelling in communion with the Divine Persons of the Holy Trinity.

As to the doctrine of transmigration, we have our Lord's own words about the man born blind, that "Neither did this man sin, nor his parents; but that the works of God should be made manifest in him" (St. John IX. 3). The difficulty could not be surmounted by the doctrine of transmigration, but it was surmounted by the Incarnation of the Divine Speaker. God designed men to be perfect as well in body as in soul and spirit (I Thess. V. 23), and Jesus Christ by becoming Man, not only showed that the body is sacred and so must be honoured and preserved as a Divine gift, but also bespoke for man a personality in heaven where all inequalities of life will be adjusted. Transmigration leads to pessimism, the Incarnation to optimism. The fundamental distinction between Christians and Hindus on this matter is that while we "groan within ourselves, waiting for our adoption, to wit, the redemption of our body" (Rom. VIII. 23), they groan within themselves, climbing the weary treadmill of transmigration, and waiting for the redemption *from* the body.

Many authors have pointed out the weak points in the idea of transmigration from Kapila downwards. If all men are one with God, this atheistical writer justly argued, then all men would gain uniformity of birth, for their conditions both mental and ethical would be identical. The memory difficulty has already been touched on, but it is greater in its moral than in its physical aspect. Reference has already been made to the unanswerable objection of another Hindu sage, quoted above, "It is not right, O prince, that the penalty of one man's action should be paid by another" (*Mahâbhârata*, XII. 32, 16). One of the indirect results of the presentment of Christianity to the Hindus, the administration of the country by Christians, and the just conduct of our Law Courts under the Indian Penal Code, i.e. the Ten Commandments writ large, is that the people are now realizing the intense importance of justice, and of that sense of fair-play which is so ingrained in every Englishman's mind. Supposing that a man was charged with murder, and it was proved that he committed the deed when in an unsound state of mind, the most illiterate coolie in the land would cry out against the injustice of hanging him. What, then, should be said of condemning a man to be born as a wolf or a rat for some supposed crime of which he was absolutely unconscious? What moral gain would there be either to the one who suffered or to those who saw such a miscarriage of justice perpetrated? The ethical standard of India is extremely low, but it is rising every day; and as a seed in a crevice will destroy the strongest tower, so will the seeds of justice overthrow in time the mighty structure that has been erected on these two unsound foundation stones of *karma* and transmigration.

The whole conception, however, hangs on the assumption that because a man is born blind a gross injustice is done, unless it is assumed that he committed some heinous sin in a former birth. But transmigration in its attempt to remove, or account for, injustice lands one in still greater injustice. There is also another consideration, and that is the principle of heredity, a scientific fact, of which the early sages knew nothing. The son of a drunkard or libertine is liable to the taint of sin, which is often transmitted to his children and grandchildren, and so the corruption of the father goes on yielding its corrupt fruit; but the grace of God is greater than the sin of man. There is no blind fatalism written on the forehead, no paralyzing burden of eighty-four lakhs of births to deaden the soul and prove an inducement to immorality; but there *is* the new birth in the God-Man Who knew no sin, which can blot out the foulest stain, and cleanse the vilest heart. Man has to suffer, no one can escape, but He too had to suffer. "Though he was a Son, yet learned obedience by the things which he suffered; and having been made perfect, he became unto all them that obey him the author of eternal salvation" (Heb. v. 8, 9).

The argument from heredity might, however, be objected to by the subtle-minded Hindu. I have insisted on the human personality of Jesus Christ and argued from analogy that the divine Personality may be known in some measure from the human. The Hindu, with his capacity for believing all manner of miracles, would raise no objection to the Virgin Birth, but he might argue that the Son of Man was stained by heredity from his human parentage. The controversy as to whether or no our Blessed Lord was exposed, e.g., to the *φρόνημα σαρκός* cannot be settled, because Revelation is silent on such subjects. But we have the plain declaration that, whatever temptation assailed Him, "He did no sin" (1 Pet. II. 22). He met His opponents with a question that effectually silenced them: "which of you convicteth me of sin?" (St. John VIII. 46). He "hath been tempted like as we are, yet without sin" (*χωρίς ἁμαρτίας*, Heb. IV. 15). His temptation must have been just as strong as ours, yet by His holy conception He was not under the irresistible dominance of sin as we are.

Before closing this chapter a few words must be said on the Hindu conception of the body. Brahma is associated illusorily with three kinds of bodies: first with the "causal" body, which when taken collectively is Îsvara, the Lord Brahmâ, or taken distributively individual souls. It may be remarked in passing that we should here have Pantheism were it not that this causal body is composed of Illusion, which nullifies the whole idea. Next, with the "subtile" or "psychic" body, composed of the five senses, the intellect, emotions, and vital airs. Thirdly, with the "gross" body, made up of various compounded elements. The intellect, with which is connected the organs of sense in the "psychic" body, is the transmigrating soul, and so is of special interest to us. In the Vêdântasâra it is called "the conventional soul," but as Dr. Banerjea has pointed out, "There can be no such thing as a substance existing *conventionally* but not *really*. . . . Conventional, as opposed to real, can only mean imaginary, in other words, false."[1] Moreover, the *summum bonum* of the Hindu is individual consciousness, and when consciousness goes there must also go with it this "psychic" body. Now, the Christian looks forward to the time when his spiritual body, animated by his own individual personality, will live

[1] See *Dialogues on the Hindu Philosophy*, by the Rev. Dr. K. M. Banerjea, p. 394; also *Hindu Pantheism*, by Col. Jacob, p. 65; and *Higher Hinduism*, by the Rev. T. E. Slater, p. 94.

on in company with the glorified body, which our Saviour now possesses, and with which He feeds the faithful, while in the physical body, in the Blessed Sacrament. Already, while we are on earth, is our body united with that glorified Body, and what would be to us a state of the greatest misery—loss of personality—becomes instead one of the most ecstatic bliss, because of the union effected through the Incarnation of our Lord. "It is sown a psychic body (*σῶμα ψυχικόν*), it is raised a spiritual body" (1 Cor. xv. 43). While we dwell below we have a foretaste of heavenly joy coupled with sacred fear as we contemplate the awful purity of God seated on His mercy-seat "in depths of burning light":—

"Oh, how I fear Thee, Living God,
With deepest, tenderest fears,
And worship Thee with trembling hope,
And penitential tears!

Yet I may love Thee too, O Lord,
Almighty as Thou art,
For Thou hast stoop'd to ask of me
The love of my poor heart."

Then, again, as we look forward to the full glory of the Beatific Vision:—

"Father of Jesus, love's reward,
What rapture will it be,
Prostrate before Thy throne to lie,
And gaze and gaze on Thee".

CHAPTER IX.

THE PATH OF SALVATION.

SOMETHING has already been said in previous chapters on the forgiveness of sin and the contrast between the Hindu and Christian conceptions of heavenly bliss; but it may be well to consider these matters in further detail, as all religions must have a final goal set before them and some method of salvation by means of which that goal may be obtained. The subject is, however, a very complex one, and we are met at the outset with the difficulty that the orthodox Hindu knows nothing of what we technically call Salvation. He has his goal and he yearns with a wearisome sadness, which we Christians can scarcely appreciate, for liberation from the endless toil of millions of re-births, yet his point of view is very different from ours. We could easily join him in his prayer:—

> "From the unreal lead me to the real,
> From darkness lead me to the light,
> From death lead me to immortality";

but we should offer the prayer in a widely different sense. To us both men and the world are only too real, while God is too often a God afar off; but to him on in comp-ing is the Supreme Being, Brahma, and Saviour n world a mere illusion. Death is to us the faithf life, whereas to him it is only one step in the Sant of a glacie of some vast mountain range to which the Himâlayas are less than an ant-hill, when every step is followed by a slip backwards, and when the air at the summit—if ever reached—is so rarefied that by it no mortal lungs can be sustained, and in it no mortal brain can remain conscious.

Following the plan adopted throughout this book of trying to thread the maze of conflicting opinions by studiously ignoring the thousand paths and bypaths which tempt us to stray, I shall keep to the main roads, having a definite journey in view and not a mere roundabout rambling in an entangling and endless jungle.

Speaking generally, Hinduism knows of no salvation except such as centres round the word Liberation, that is release from the repetition of births. But this, of course, was unknown during the Vêdic period, for transmigration belongs to the mediaeval period. It leads its followers along the Path of the Fathers, and then along the Path of the Gods; first to the personal Lord, Brahmâ, and then to the impersonal and supreme Brahma. Afterwards when the doctrine of the identity of the Absolute Self and the individual self grows more clear and definite, it shows that the approach of the human to the Divine is an impossibility, for they are already united, in spite of ignorance, in a perfect oneness; and therefore salvation consists in nothing more than the lightning-flash which reveals this complete identity.

According to the Vêdic idea the Oriental phrase, "O king, live for ever," seems to sum up the pious aspiration of the early sages. Provided that the rains fell, the sun shone, children were numerous, cattle strong and healthy, and crops abundant, what more could anyone reasonably demand? Death was the enemy to avoid, life was the period to enjoy, and the life after death was a thing unknown. Eat and drink, dance and sing, and let death be buried under a mountain!

"Go hence, O Death, pursue thy special pathway,
  Apart from that which gods are wont to travel.
To Thee I say it who hast eyes and hearest:
  Touch not our offspring, injure not our heroes.

As ye have come effacing Mrityu's footstep,
  To further times prolonging your existence,
May ye be rich in children and possessions,
  Cleansed, purified, and meet for sacrificing.

Divided from the dead are these, the living:
  Now be our calling on the gods successful;
We have gone forth for dancing and for laughter,
  To further times prolonging our existence.

Here I erect this rampart to the living;
  Let none of those, none other, reach this limit.
May they survive a hundred lengthened autumns,
  And may they bury Death beneath this mountain."

(*Rig Vêda*, X. 18, I.)

But the orthodox Hinduism of to-day, as I have said before, is not based on the Vêdas, but upon the Upanishads, and again, not so much on the Upanishads as on the "Targums" of the commentators. In these there are many words giving different shades of meaning to denote the general idea of liberation such as *mukti* and *moksha*, deliverance from re-births, or freedom from Prakriti, i.e. matter; *kaivalya*, absolute solitude; and *nirvâna*, extinction, or absorption into the Supreme. These demand some consideration, especially the distinction between the purely Hindu idea of *mukti* and the Buddhistic conception of *nirvâna*. *Mukti* and *moksha* are both derived from the same Sanskrit root, and denote deliverance, or emancipation. Though Christians have adopted the latter word for heaven, neither word means anything but deliverance from the curse of repeated births and their attendant miseries. We Christians lament that "we are tied and bound with the chain of our sins," and long to be loosed by the pitifulness of God's great mercy; and daily do we also pray that He will "deliver us from the Evil one," but no corresponding chord is struck in the Hindu's heart. What the latter aspires to is riddance from repeated births, endless miseries, physical evils, all the perplexities and problems of life, and the cravings of unsatisfied desires, as well as from the envy, hatred, malice, and all uncharitableness which embitter men's dealings with their friends and kinsfolk.

"When all the wishes that here lie hidden in his heart now cease, then mortal man becomes immortal, and is united with the Brahma Itself. When once all the knots, that here below are in his heart, are disentangled, then mortal becomes immortal. Here endeth the pious teaching" (*Kath. Upanishad*, II. 6, 14). To get rid of these "knots of the heart" the orthodox Hindu is quite willing to forfeit all the positive blessings of individual humanity, all personality and all self-consciousness. Nehemiah Goreh, who belonged to the straitest sect of the Brâhmans, when quoting the Psalm (CXLVI. 1, 2) "Praise ye the LORD. Praise the LORD, O my soul. While I live will I praise the LORD: I will sing praises unto my GOD *while I have any being*," says, "I, as a Christian, have been taught to believe that to love and glorify GOD is the very end of my existence. In this will consist my eternal joy and happiness. Not so was my faith when a Hindu. The state of salvation, according to my belief at that time, was to be free from transmigration, and to be separated, not only from the body, but even from the *antakarana*, which is the organ of all our thoughts and consciousness, and to remain unconscious for ever."[1]

As illustrating the way in which human personality is dissolved, and individual self-consciousness is extinguished by absorption into the impersonal Brahma, the following passage may be quoted:—

"As rivers streaming fall into the ocean losing their name and form, even so a wise man, giving up name and form, enters the Divine, the highest universal Spirit" (*Mund. Upanishad*, IV. 2, 8).

[1] *Supposed and real doctrines of Hinduism*, p. 29.

According to the atheistic school of Sânkhya, liberation is gained by the separation of Self and matter. It will be remembered that in this system we have two constituents, the Soul (*Purusha*) and matter (*Prakriti*). Now all pain comes by association with the latter, and when one can escape from its grasp, or from its *uphâdis* (the products and trappings of life which limit the conditions of the body), then one attains to absolute isolation, or aloneness (*kaivalya*). Whenever Prakriti ceases to work then the person learns his own nature and realizes that he is completely different from matter :—

"The dissolution, in the inverse order, of the qualities, bereft of action for the Self (Purusha), is *Kaivalya*, or it is the establishment of the power of knowledge in its own nature" (*Yoga Sutra*, IV. 33).

This liberation must end in complete loss of personality and self-consciousness, for both these are products of matter, and must therefore be extinguished in the act of liberation. As there is no Self, into which the lower self may be absorbed, *kaivalya* denotes a state of unconsciousness indistinguishable from blank nothingness. Such must be the end of any atheistic philosophy.

Passing by all minor distinctions, let us now consider the difference between the *mukti*, or absorption into Brahma, and *nirvâna*, the corresponding doctrine of Buddhism. "The highest good," according to the teaching of the Bhagavad Gîtâ, is absorption, which is practically extinction. As a lamp is extinguished and the flame vanishes, so does the human soul become extinct in the impersonal God. Thus we read:—

"As the waters fall into the sea, which, though filled, continues within its limits, so he only, into whom all desires are withdrawn, obtains tranquillity, but not he who cherishes desires. The man who, giving up all desires lives without desire, without self-interest, and without selfishness, he obtains tranquillity. This is the condition of Brahma, O son of Pritha. Having attained to this, a man is no more deluded; and if a man continues in this to the hour of death, he obtains extinction in the Brahma" (*Bhagavad Gîtâ*, XI. 70-72).

Extinction is thus the highest bliss, the supreme salvation.

The following description may also be quoted:—

"Now having entered into blissful Brahma, I am just as a cool lake in hot summer: I am in peace, in course of being extinguished, and in lonely comfort" (*Mahâbhârata*, XII. 177, 48).

Here it is the act of extinction that is so delightful. In England we give a person the "cold shoulder" when we dislike him, but in India we give a "cool glance" to the person whom we love best, for in that land of fiery heat it is ever coolness that we long for, and "the shadow of a great rock in a weary land".

When we use the word *nirvâna*, we almost always associate it with the Buddhist conception, and so we must ask what the Buddha really taught. It must never be forgotten that, though Sakya Muni started as a reformer of orthodox Hinduism, he ended as a practical atheist, very far from his first starting place. He ignored the supreme Self and denied the existence of any self in man; so that *nirvâna* from his point of view meant nothing, and could mean nothing, but annihilation.[1] He was silent on the subject of eschatology, for what was there that he could possibly have said? The modern Buddhist, to whom *nirvâna* is the abode of all bliss, and the English reader who revels in Edwin Arnold's *Light of Asia*, will of course deny this; but we have here only another illustration of the oft-repeated truth that the human heart will not be put off with negative abstractions, and so manufactures for itself positive and concrete joys. Gautama might deny the possibility of God's existence, but that does not prevent his followers from seating him on a throne as god. He might deny the possibility of a soul, immortality and a resurrection, but that is no reason why Buddhists should not enjoy by anticipation all the pleasures and raptures of a state of bliss in heaven. As a matter of hard fact there is nothing to choose between the position of the orthodox Brâhman and that of the Buddhist. For absorption into an impersonal Essence with complete loss of individual personality and self-consciousness only differs from absolute annihilation in the matter of terminology.

[1] "Annihilation, then, as regards individuals, is as much the ultimate destiny of the soul as it is of the body, and '*Not to be*' is the melancholy result of the religion and philosophy of the Hindus" (*Essays on the Religion of the Hindus*, by Wm. Wilson, II. 114).

But adopting the Hindu's view that the attainment of Brahmahood is the *summum bonum* of existence, I must, at the risk of wearying my reader, go back again for a moment to the difference between the masculine Brahmâ and the neuter Brahma. The Path of the Fathers leads up to the former, the Îshvara, or Lord of the Vêdânta, but that journey always ends with a return to more births; whereas the Path of the gods leads to the impersonal Essence, from which there can be no possibility of return. The difference between Brahma and Brahmâ may seem to us fanciful and wanting in reality; but to the Hindu the distinction is of vital importance. Human personality is limited in all directions. Not only is the black, thick-lipped negro of Africa different from the wheat-coloured and refined Âryan, but we are all different from our own brothers and sisters in a dozen different ways, just as every leaf on a tree differs from every other leaf. Our features, our gestures, even the tones of our voices are often quite distinct. Moreover, just as it is impossible for the Ethiopian to change his skin, so it is impossible for us to escape from the limitations and idiosyncrasies of our own personalities. And if our personality limits us, must not personality also limit the supreme Being? This was the difficulty that the orthodox Hindus have always felt. They could tolerate no idea of limitation, or of what is conditional, in their conception of the Godhead. Everything that savoured of humanity, or personality, was to them an impossibility. Granted that the Deity be One-without-a-second then it follows there can be nothing finite; and *a fortiori* there cannot be two Infinites. The One Supreme Self is boundless, unlimited, unconditioned and without attributes, parts or qualities; whereas human personality is never able to free itself from conditions and limits.

If it is urged that such subtleties only affect the speculative mind of the oriental sage, we shall do well to remember that few men of our time were more practical and hard-headed than the late Archbishop Temple. Yet hear what he said:—

"There is a sense in which we cannot ascribe personality to the unknown absolute Being; for our personality is of necessity compassed with limitations, and from these limitations we find it impossible to separate our conception of person. When we speak of God as a person, we cannot but acknowledge that this personality far transcends our conceptions. . . . If to deny personality to Him is to assimilate Him to a blind and dead rule, we cannot but repudiate such denial altogether. If to deny personality to Him is to assert His incomprehensibility, we are ready at once to acknowledge our weakness and incapacity."[1]

With our anthropomorphic conceptions of God, we English people are apt to transfer our conceptions of personality to the Most High without realizing how infinitely superior He is to us, and how high above all our limitations His divine Personality must be placed. The Hindu, on the other hand, with his intense awe

[1] *Bampton Lectures*, by Archbishop Temple, p. 57.

for the transcendence of the supreme Self has refined his conception of Him again, and yet again, till he has merged the Lord Brahmâ into Brahma, and then sublimated Brahma till nothing is left save abstract Existence. Ineffable awe, remorseless logic, and the most daring flights into the region of speculative mysticism carried the sage higher and higher till God and man, heaven and earth, vanished into thin air and nothing remained but the shadow of a shade. To realize one's identity with, and to be swallowed up into, that ghost of a shadow is the Hindu's conception of what we Christians call Salvation.

And now as we follow the soul in its upward path, we must bear certain facts in mind lest we lose ourselves in the maze of speculation. We shall not have to deal with the scriptures, either inspired (*sruti*) or uninspired (*smriti*), so much as with the opinions of the commentators. Râmânuja keeps us more than Sankara on the lower path of Brahmâ, while the latter often fluctuates so much between Brahmâ and Brahma, that it is almost impossible to know to which he refers. Lastly, as said above, when the doctrine of the Vêdânta had fully developed, the human self was considered incapable of progressing either towards the lower Brahmâ or the higher Brahma, because it had already realized its complete identity with the Supreme.

The ancient poets who composed the Vêdas were not troubled with any eschatological problems. They believed that those who had led a virtuous life would go with new and perfected bodies to the realm of Yama.

In the funeral hymn quoted in the last chapter they apostrophized the soul departing to their forefathers. There they were to associate with the two kings Yama and Varuna. All their desires were to be fulfilled. There having abandoned all sin they were to be at home clothed with radiant bodies. It will be noticed that there is here a distinct advance beyond the old idea of burying death under a mountain. In another hymn Soma, the moon, is implored to grant immortality:—

"Where there is imperishable light, in the world where the sun is placed, in that immortal, eternal world place me, O Soma.

"Where Vaivasvata (Yama) is king, where there is the descent (or, the interior) of heaven, where the ever-flowing waters are, there make me immortal, O Soma.

"Where one moves as one listeth, in the third light, the third heaven of heaven, where every place is full of light, there make me immortal, O Soma.

"Where there are all wishes and desires, where the red sun culminates, where there are offerings and enjoyment, there make me immortal, O Soma.

"Where there are delights and pleasures, where joys and enjoyments dwell, where the wishes of the heart are fulfilled, there make me immortal, O Soma."[1]

(*Rig Vêda*, IX. 113, 7.)

In another hymn we revert more to the original idea of the next world being a glorified reproduction of

[1] Translation by Max Müller.

earth. We read there, in the *Athara Vêda*, of cows, soft winds, cooling rain, cakes of ghî (butter), rivers running with milk and honey, and numbers of women, all intended for the enjoyment of the departed.

By the time we have reached the Upanishads we are in an entirely different atmosphere. The following passage shows how the soul proceeds along the path of the Fathers (*Pitriyâna*). Several different accounts are given in different Upanishads, but this will probably serve our purpose best:—

"Those who in their village practise charity as sacrifice and pious works, go to the smoke, from smoke to night, from night to the other (waning) half of the moon, from the other half of the moon to the six months when the sun moves to the South. But they do not reach the year. From the months they go to the world of the Fathers, from the world of Fathers to the ether, from the ether to the moon. That is Soma the king. That is the food of the gods, the gods feed on it. Having tarried there, as long as there is a rest (of works), they return again on the way on which they came, to the ether, from the ether to the air (*vâyu*). When he has become air he becomes smoke, having become smoke he becomes mist, having become mist he becomes a cloud, having become a cloud he rains down. Then they are born as rice and corn, herbs and trees, sesamum and beans. From thence the escape is very difficult. For whoever they are who eat that food and scatter seed, he becomes like unto them. Those whose conduct has been good will probably attain some good birth, the birth of a Brâhman, or a Kshatriya, or a Vaisya. But those whose conduct has been evil will probably attain an evil birth, the birth of a dog, or a hog, or a chandâla (Pariah)." [1]

Such an account sounds very childish to us, but it is of interest in showing how the child-races, unaided by revelation, try to explain difficult problems to themselves. The subtle essence of the simple villager who has done his round of pious works escapes after death to the moon, returns by rain, and enters the womb of woman or beast by means of food. The same Upanishad tells us that those who have done evil, i.e. broken caste laws, etc., do not proceed either to the path of the Fathers or that of the gods. "On neither of these two roads do these small oft-returning creatures proceed. Theirs is the third state, of which it is said, 'Live and die'." Thus low-caste people, evildoers, and animals go round and round in an endless succession of births with no other rule of life but "let us eat and drink for to-morrow we die". How they ever attain to the second rank of life is not explained. Now let us look at the first-class people who pursue the Path of the gods (*Dêvayâna*).

"Those who know this, and those who in the forest follow austerity as faith, go to the light (*arkis*), from light to day, from day to the waxing half of the moon to the six months when the sun goes to the North, from

[1] *Chhândogya Upanishad*, translated by Max Müller, Gifford Lectures, p. 119. A similar passage from the *Brihaddâr Upanishad* has already been quoted in the chapter on Karma and Transmigration.

the six months when the sun goes to the North to the year, from the year to the sun, from the sun to the moon, from the moon to the lightning. There is a person, not a man, he leads them to Brahma. This is the Path of the Gods."

Thus, those who have led the "religious" life escape from the region of *sâṃsâra*, or corporeal existence, they have passed beyond the realm of Brahmâ, and are in no further dread of returning to earth.

In another Upanishad, too long to quote, we have a detailed description of the path by which the advanced soul proceeds on his journey. When he has arrived at the moon, she asks him the question, "Who art thou?" If he gives her the correct answer she sets him free; but if not he must again return to the earth by rain. In the latter case he prays, "Raise me now in a vigorous man, and pour me through a vigorous man into a mother". In the former case he tells the moon who he is, ending up with the declaration, "I am thou". Then she allows him to proceed along the Path of the gods and to the realm of Brahma. As he approaches, Brahma commands, "Run towards him with such worship as is due to Myself. He has reached the river *vigarâ* (ageless), he will never age." Thereupon five hundred Apsaras (beautiful maidens) adorn him with garments and garlands, anoint him and perfume him, and then regale him with fruit. Then he crosses the river Vigarâ, by which he attains perpetual youth, and gets rid of his deeds, bestowing his good ones on the relatives whom he loves best, and his evil ones on those whom he hates. He passes on to the palace of Brahma whom he realizes step by step by his odour, his flavour, his splendour, and his glory. The door-keepers, Indra and Prajâpathi, flee at his approach. At last as he draws near to the throne, he sees Brahma reclining on his couch, and he mounts it first with one foot. "Who art thou?" demands Brahma, and he shall answer, "I am a season, and the child of the seasons, sprung from the womb of endless space, the seed of the wife, the light of the year, the self of all that is. Thou art the Self of all that is; what Thou art, that am I"[1] (*Kaushîtaki Upanishad*, I. 2).

I have placed the passages in this order to illustrate the gradual evolution of ideas in broad outline; but the commentators on the scriptures, while practically ignoring the Vêdas, decline to admit that there can be any progress in the inspired writings, or that one Upanishad can be inferior to another, however conflicting the accounts may be. This naturally leads them into all manner of difficulties, and they make desperate efforts to reconcile these inconsistencies. We need not follow them as they plough the sands, but one or two points may be given to show in what direction their difficulties lie.

Liberation may be pursued by many different methods, such as sacrificial works, the attainment of knowledge, asceticism, self-mortification, yoga-practices,

[1] The full translation will be found in the Gifford Lectures, pp. 120-23.

the use of the sacred OM, instruction by a guru, and the devotion known as *bhakti*. Still the end, as we know, is the same—the attainment of the knowledge of identity with Brahma. But the difficulty at once presents itself: When does the human soul attain that knowledge? While living on earth? After death? After millions of re-births while in the region of Brahmâ? Or, at the final consummation when Brahmahood is attained? Liberation implies no change in the nature of this human soul, either moral or otherwise, but simply the knowledge of its identity with Brahma. Now, the attainment of this knowledge must be an instantaneous act, a perception made once for all; and whoever gains this knowledge, at whatever stage of his life, is *ipso facto* liberated. We are distinctly told of the "liberated but still living" that:—

"The 'liberated but still living' is he who by knowing the impartite Brahma, which is his own essence, a result brought about by the removal of the ignorance enveloping It, perceives It clearly as the Impartite and his own essence; and, in consequence of the removal of Ignorance and its effects, such as accumulated works, doubt, and error, remains intent on Brahma, freed from all fetters. . . . On arising from meditation, though he sees that, by his body which is the receptacle of flesh, blood, etc.—by his organs, which are the seat of blindness, slowness, etc.—and by his internal organ, which is the seat of hunger, thirst, sorrow, etc.—works are being done according to the previous bent of each, . . . he regards them not as real because they have been cancelled. Just as one watching what he knows to be a conjuring performance does not regard it as a reality."[1]

But Sankara, the chief commentator, has already told us that at the moment of liberation all *uphâdis* disappear, i.e. the limiting conditions such as body, senses, sense-objects and perception. Here we are in a hopeless state of dilemma; for either the body must die, or these *uphâdis* must continue to exist. Sankara tries to get out of the difficulty by adopting the usual Indian device: he gives a simile instead of an argument. As a potter's wheel continues to rotate after the completion of the pot, so the body continues to exist after liberation has been attained. But as liberation *ipso facto* destroys the *uphâdis* of the body, so, to make the two cases parallel, the completion of the pot ought to cause the wheel to fly into atoms, and how then could it continue rotating? Then there is another similar objection. At the moment of liberation "all works disappear". So long as life continues—and it might continue twenty or thirty years—it is obvious that actions must continue. Sankara is ready with another illustration. Owing to some defect of the eyes a man may see two moons, and after a successful operation he may for some time continue to see double. This, again, is no answer, as Sankara knew quite well, so he ends authoritatively with, "This is no subject for dispute. For how could a man who in the conviction of

[1] *Vêdântasâra* (34), by Col. Jacob, pp. 121, 2.

his heart knows himself to be Brahma—though he is still in the body—be refuted by another?"

Take another comment. "When the false vestures of the body fall, the sage enters completely into the Godhead as water unites with water, air with air, and fire with fire." So says Sankara. But the individual self and the Absolute Self are always identical, though owing to *avidyâ* the human self is not aware of its identity. This, replies Sankara, is like a maid who has lost her necklace, and while she is searching for it she happens to put her hand to her neck and, behold, it has been there all the while! This is very pretty, but it does not help us to solve the problem of the body and its "false vestures," the *uphâdis*.

In a previous chapter I referred to the popular ideas of final happiness. There are three lower stages and one higher: (1) Being in the same world as the personal God (*Sâlokya*); (2) dwelling near the God (*Sâmîpya*); (3) having the same form (*Sârûpya*); and (4) union with the supreme Brahma (*Sâyujya*). When once the *uphâdis* have fallen off and no longer hamper the self with their delusive vestures, then sin, though still possible, can leave no stain:—

"As no water sticks to the leaf of the lotus flower, so the sinful deed does not stick to him who knows this" (*Chhândogya Upanishad*, IV. 143).

Again, "As the reed burns if thrown into the fire, all the sins of him who knows this are burned. In the sage who knows himself as the Brahma, the fire itself burns and consumes the sinful deeds of the past and present."

Good deeds as well as ill cause a repetition of births, and liberation is impossible till the fruits of these good deeds have been "eaten":—

"The Self is a wall, a boundary line, that these worlds may not be confounded. Neither day nor night, nor old age, death and pain, nor good deeds, nor evil deeds overstep that wall. All sins retreat before it, for that Brahma-world is free from sins" (*Chhând. Upan.*, VIII. 4, 1).

We Christians hold that "There shall in no wise enter into it (i.e. the holy city) anything unclean, or he that maketh an abomination and a lie" (Rev. XXI. 27); but it is difficult for us to understand why good deeds should shut anyone outside the wall. Another difficulty is that the commentators do not fix any boundary line of their own. At one moment we are in the lower world of Brahmâ, the Îshvara, from which the word *Aisvarya* (the heavenly glory) is derived, at the next we are in the realm of the higher Brahma, which practically means extinction. At one time the pious one is a Brâhman on earth, at another he is an unconscious essence merging into the impersonal, unconscious Essence. Now we have the glory of every desire fulfilled, and the glory of dominion with Brahmâ; again we have the state of that beyond dreamless sleep, when the pious soul is swallowed up in Brahma and vanishes like the flame of a candle when extinguished. Sankara strives hard to reconcile all these contradictions—for are they not all found in the inspired pages of the Upanishads?—and yet clings with all his might to the higher esoteric views of the union with Brahma. Râmânuja is more contented with the lower plane in accordance with the following scripture:—

"Whatever aims he may aspire to, whatever wish he may cherish, through his mere desire it comes and in its possession he is satisfied" (*Chhând. Upan.*, VIII. 2).

So long as men are men with men's hearts and men's emotions and passions, they will necessarily crave for the fellowship of their relatives, for flowers and odours, fruit and wine, song and dance, and above all for the smiles of women. What if these joys do belong to the world of the lower Brahmâ; and what if Brahmâ himself has to be swallowed up at the end of each *kalpa*, or æon? The strongest philosophy and the subtlest metaphysics of men's intellects are but as green withes to bind the Samson of men's human desires. Samson has only to shake himself, and the bonds will fall from him as "tow that smelleth the fire".

To establish a link between pagan philosophy and the Incarnation something must now be said about the history of the word Logos. Prof. Max Müller writes: "It may be truly said that the founders of the religions of the world have all been bridge-builders".[1] We have seen how the departed Hindu cannot approach Brahma when on the Path of the gods without crossing the river which separates him from Brahma.

[1] See the Gifford Lectures, XII. *passim*.

"In him the heaven, the earth, and the sky are woven, the mind also with all the senses. Know Him alone as the Self, and leave off other names. He is the bridge of the Immortal, i.e. the bridge by which we reach our own immortality" (*Mund. Upan.*, II. 2, 5).

May not we also say that the incarnate Logos must be both God, with one foot in heaven, and Man with the other foot on earth? According to the interpretation of the distinguished translator of the Sacred Books of the East, the word Brahma comes from the root *brih* (*verbum*, word); and it in its neuter form is *τὸ ὄντως ὄν*, the propelling force of the universe, while in its masculine form Brahmâ it is the creator of the world. According to the Greek philosophy which Philo adopted, Logos means "word embodied in sound". "Nothing," says Max Müller, when commenting on Philo's philosophy, "could supply a better simile for God thinking and uttering the cosmos than the act of man in thinking and uttering his thought." When Philo speaks of the Thought or Word of God realized in the visible world, the ideal creation, he adopts the phrase *υἱὸς μονογενής* to describe this Logos. And if St. John adopted these words from Philo, it was because the unique Son, Jesus Christ, was rather the Word of God incarnate in the true sense of the term Logos than in the sense of the Son of the Blessed Virgin.

Another point to notice is that though the Brâhman boldly claims that "What Thou art, that am I," still he has the greatest horror of the Supreme Being coming into contact with, or being limited by, the gross material world. The Jew looked up to Yahveh as a Being so awful and so far transcending man and matter, that he did not dare even to pronounce His sacred Name. Philo, however, "combines the awful reverence of the Semitic with the philosophical sobriety of the Greek". The divine Wisdom by which God conceived the world of ideas is allowed "to come into contact with gross matter as little as God Himself. That contact is brought about by the Logos, as a bond which is to unite heavenly and earthly things and to transfer the intellectual creation from the divine mind upon matter." Once more, "Philo was satisfied with having found in the Greek Logos what he and many with him were looking for, the bridge between the human and the Divine, which had been broken in religion by the inapproachableness of Jehovah, and in philosophy by the incompatibility between the absolute Being and phenomenal world".

Bishop Westcott, however, does not admit that St. John in the opening verses of his Gospel borrowed from Philo. The word Logos admits of two meanings, Reason and Thought, and "when Philo speaks of 'the divine Logos' his thought is predominantly of the divine Reason, and not of the divine Word. . . . The conception of a divine Word, that is of a divine Will sensibly manifested in personal action is not naturally derived from that of a divine Reason."[1] The word *Memra* as used in Palestine means Word only, and is the term adopted by St. John. "Philo occupied him-

[1] Introduction to the Gospel of St. John, p. xvi.

self with the abstract conception of the divine Intelligence, and so laid the foundations of a philosophy. The Palestinian instinct seized upon the concrete idea of 'the Word of God,' as representing His personal action, and unconsciously prepared the way for a Gospel of the Incarnation. St. John started from the conception of 'the Word'; and by this means in the end he gave reality to the conception of 'the Reason'."

This brings us to the opening words of the Fourth Gospel:—

"In the beginning was the Word, and the Word was with God, and the Word was God. The same was in the beginning with God. All things were made by him; and without him was not anything made that hath been made. In him was life; and the life was the light of men. And the light shineth in the darkness; and the darkness apprehended it not" (St. John I. 1-6). Thus the Word was with God in closest union (*sâyujya*) and was eternally God in His essential Nature. "Creation itself was (in some sense) the result of the eternal fellowship expressed in the relation of the Word to God," writes the Bishop. The Word was the mediate Agent of creation through whom all the phenomenal world came into being. "And the Word became flesh (ὁ λόγος σὰρξ ἐγένετο), and dwelt among us (*sâlokya*) (and we beheld his glory, glory as of the only-begotten from the Father), full of grace and truth." And this same Jesus "being in the form of God (*sârûpya*) . . . being made in the likeness of men . . . humbled himself, becoming obedient even unto death, yea, the death of the Cross. Wherefore God also highly exalted him, and gave unto him the name which is above every name; that in the name of Jesus every knee should bow" (Phil. II. 7, 10). Here then we have the Path of the gods leading to the *summum bonum* of Christianity. The Incarnate Son is the divine Bridge. By our sacramental union while on earth, before we have shaken off the *uphâdis* of the body we have already got possession of "eternal life," a positive gift. We are already "members of Christ, children of God, and inheritors of the kingdom of heaven". This is our path of salvation, and from it there is no return. The phrase "the Word became flesh" is absolutely unique, and is one of the "great sentences" of the Bible. "The unity of the Lord's Person is preserved before and after the Incarnation. His Personality is divine. Still His humanity is really complete. He remaining the same Person as before did not simply assume humanity as something which could be laid aside: He *became flesh*. He did not simply become 'a man' but 'man'."[1]

Our Lord's Incarnation is essentially a different thing from the *avatârs* of Vishnu. The latter never professed to serve any other purpose than to remedy abuses in the world and had nothing to do with salvation. Hence the two cannot be compared. The comparison only exists between Jesus Christ and Brahma, or Brahmâ. Jesus did not become a Person through His Incarnation, for eternally He is one of the Persons

[1] Bishop Westcott, *ad loc.*

of the Blessed Trinity. He was not an Essence or principle descending temporarily upon man; but He is completely, universally, really and permanently Man. Yet He is eternally God, and God cannot die. On the cross, and in the grave, He is still the living God. As God He raised man's fallen nature, and it is as God that He forgives sin and saves us in the fullest sense. As Man He offered Himself as a sacrifice for all humanity, for "apart from shedding of blood there is no remission" (Heb. IX. 22). By becoming flesh the two perfect Natures were combined in one Person. As a Person He is not limited as we are, and we only use the term Person, as we do such other terms as "Son of God," so as to bring divine and mysterious truths into the limits of our human language and human comprehension. Still, on the other hand, we cannot speak of Him as impersonal, or as an Essence like Brahma, for He uses the word "man" (*ἄνθρωπος*) in St. John VIII. 40, "ye seek to kill me, a man," etc. St. Paul also speaks of Him as "one mediator also between God and men, himself man" (I Tim. II. 5). Looking at the matter from this point of view we see what was the *crux* of all the difficulties of the Hindus. They shrank from any possible curtailment of the majesty of God by hampering the Infinite with finite conditions and limitations. And so they evolved the conception of the One-without-a-second. Then starting out with this conception of the Deity they rigidly drew their logical conclusions and so fell into those multifarious and complex errors of which Hinduism consists. Their major premiss is false, and so all their conclusions are necessarily false. To put the case in another way, orthodox Hinduism is like a vast tent supported by a single pole; and when that pole snaps the tent collapses on the heads of those who have pitched it with such immense labour. Our Lord did, then, just that thing which every Hindu conceived to be impossible: by taking man's flesh He, as Man, reconciled the finite and the Infinite. He united the Supreme with the phenomenal world without detracting from the glory of the Godhead. While remaining transcendent God, high above all created beings, He is also immanent in the world, for ever Man. He brought to earth a golden key by which He showed men how their stubborn locks may be opened. No wonder that the angels sang for joy when they realized that those mysteries, which they and the prophets had groped after in vain —however diligent their search—were at last to be revealed (1 St. Peter 1. 10-13). And let us pay all honour to the Hindu sages, although their scriptures may seem at times to us to be such unintelligible jargon, and at times so childish; for what zeal have they displayed! They failed, as they were bound to fail, with the dim light which alone was theirs, but still they searched as no other nation on the face of the earth has ever searched, into the deepest mysteries of the supreme Being.

It is impossible, as it would be undesirable, to go into all the countless ways in which the Incarnation enters into the life of the individual soul and that of the Church; but it will suffice to mention a few points of importance which most nearly touch on the subject of this essay. First, Christ, ἄνωθεν ἐρχόμενος (St. John III. 31), is the "second Man" who is of heaven (1 Cor. XV. 47); and He inaugurated a new race in distinction from that of the first Adam who is "of the earth, earthy". "He is the head of the body, the church . . . the beginning (ἀρχή as the Father is πηγή) and the firstborn" (Col. I. 18; and cf. Rom. VIII. 29). As the character of the Incarnate is that of One "full of grace and truth," so Christ imparts not only salvation to the individual, but also infuses into His body, the Church, the grace and virtue of His humanity (Eph. I. 22, 3). The Church has not only faith, but shows its faith by its works.

Men's evil deeds are washed away in the blood of the Lamb that was slain, while their good works follow them. His Spirit is their source.

> "And so the Word had breath, and wrought
> With human hands the creed of creeds,
> In loveliness of perfect deeds,
> More strong than all poetic thought."
>
> (*In Memoriam.*)

Primarily, liberation meant for the Jews deliverance from slavery and all its attendant miseries; but when Zacharias announced that the God of Israel had "raised up a horn of salvation for us," then he introduced a new and grander idea, "the knowledge of salvation unto his people in the remission of their sins" (St.

Luke I. 69, 77). Jesus Christ, then, effected liberation for the saints by delivering them from the power of sin, of death, and of Satan by the remission of sins, by propitiation, and by reconciliation with GOD. This, then, is salvation to the Christian, coupled with the gift of "eternal life" both in this world and the next. Finally, the Incarnation will be completed when all Christ's enemies, including death, have been put in subjection under His feet (I Cor. XV. 27). He will not be swallowed up like Brahmâ into Brahma at the end of each æon (*kalpa*); but "the Son also himself will be subjected to him that did subject all things unto him, that GOD may be all in all" (v. 28). Then the great voices will proclaim: "The kingdom of the world is become the kingdom of our Lord, and of his Christ: and he shall reign for ever and for ever" (Rev. XI. 15).

This chapter might fitly have ended here, but unfortunately a fresh difficulty has now to be faced.

. . . .

It may be urged that the whole doctrine of the Incarnation is invalidated, or at any rate weakened, by the recent attack on the Virgin Birth. Is this theory that the Son of Man was not necessarily born of a Virgin mother valid? Is the doctrine of the Virgin Birth nothing more than a pious opinion? Is it, or is it not, essential to the doctrine of the Incarnation? The author of *The New Theology* writes: "The credibility and significance of Christianity are in no way affected by the doctrine of the Virgin Birth otherwise than that it tends to put a barrier between Jesus and the race, and to make Him something that cannot properly be called human". The new theology of England begins to bear in several respects a close resemblance to the old theology of India, and not least in this. The Hindu may ask with quite as much force as our modernist theologians, "If your Jesus was born in the ordinary way of two human parents how is He any better than our Krishna?" For myself I could give no answer to his objection. Either the Church has been right from the second century downwards in professing its belief that He was "conceived by the Holy Ghost, born of the Virgin Mary," or else the Christian faith has been established on an unsafe foundation. The present Bishop of Oxford has declared that "There are no believers in the Incarnation discoverable who are not believers in the Virgin Birth".[1] And experience bears him out. The two doctrines stand or fall together. And Bishop Westcott, who has taught us all so much about the importance of this central doctrine of our faith, also wrote of one who called the Virgin Birth in question: "He makes the Lord a man, one man in the race, and not the New Man, Son of Man, in Whom the race is gathered up. He makes the Lord's personality human —a fatal error." On Christmas Day we declare that Almighty God gave His "only-begotten Son to take our nature upon him, and as at this time to be born of a pure Virgin"; and again, He gave Jesus Christ

[1] *Dissertations*, by Bishop Gore, p. 48.

His "only Son to be born as at this time for us, who by the operation of the Holy Ghost was made very man of the substance of the Virgin Mary, His mother". If this is not true how are we better than Nestorian heretics or Krishna devotees? If it be maintained that Jesus Christ might have taken man's nature upon Him by some other method than the one which has been held by the Catholic Church, *semper, ubique, et ab omnibus*, then we have a right to ask what that method may be. No other method which we can conceive of is comparable with the one which we hold either in naturalness or in doctrinal importance. Hindus never stumble at miracles, or oppose Christianity on this head. The life of our Lord was one series of miracles from His Birth to His Ascension; and this miracle of the Holy Ghost's operation, stupendous though it be, is more simple, more natural, and more appropriate than any other method that we know or can think of. If any such method were discovered, Christianity which has stood on this as one of its foundation-stones for well-nigh two milleniums, would not be Christianity at all, but some other entirely different religion.

The historical critic of to-day, exaggerating the importance of his own branch of research, and minimizing the other equally important gifts belonging to the one body with its many members, demands that the faculty of faith which is higher than mere reason, the belief of the creeds, the testimony of the undivided Catholic Church, and the sweet reasonableness of the Gospel story, which has satisfied the hearts as well as the minds of millions of the faithful, should give place to some fine-spun spider-thread theory which is anything but Christianity. "Is the evidence true?" we are authoritatively asked, and are straightway haled before the modern Cæsar. Then we are confronted with "difficulties" which are no difficulties at all except in the minds of those who have started with some preconceived theory about miracles, and then have striven to force everything into this same mould of their own fashioning. While protesting against such one-sided methods, let us accept the challenge and stand before Cæsar.

First of all then, there are the two plain statements of St. Matthew and St. Luke, clearly independent in origin, but derived, of course, from the Blessed Mother herself and indirectly from Joseph. St. Matthew's statement was sufficient to set at rest in the minds of the Jews any breath of scandal that might have suggested itself as regards the purity of the meek mother of God, who had faith enough to place her will in submission to the divine Will. St. Luke, who took such pains to make inquiries as to the facts on which he based his history, gives equally unmistakable evidence, manifestly derived at first hand from the mother herself. St. Mark, who begins with the baptism and public ministry of our Lord, incidentally supports the case of the Virgin Birth when he quotes the objection of the Jews, "Is not this the carpenter, the Son of Mary?" (VI. 3; compare this with St. Matt. XIII. 55). To argue that St. John knew nothing of the Virgin

Birth when he almost certainly had the other Gospels before him, and when his opponent, the arch-heretic Cerinthus, knew the story and impugned its truth, looks almost like shutting one's eyes to facts. If the story of the other Evangelists was incredible, could he on the grounds of honesty have allowed it to pass without making some kind of protest? When the Jews made their *ad hominem* retort, "We (ἡμεῖς emphatic) were not born of fornication" (VIII. 41), is it conceivable that St. John was ignorant of the Jewish scandal when he placed the words on record?[1]

But the historical critic assures us that St. Paul knew nothing of the Virgin Birth. Now, first, the argument from silence is of all arguments the most unsafe, and the least likely to carry weight except in the mind of one already obsessed with some preconceived idea. And, secondly, St. Paul does give us indirect evidence, which may in the circumstances be of greater value than a direct statement. If he had not known and believed the story of the Virgin Birth, that grand passage of his about the entrance of sin into the world through Adam, contrasted with the grace which entered through Jesus Christ would fall quite flat and pointless (Rom. V. 12-21). If "Christ came," as Tertullian says, "to consecrate a new order of birth," then the argument is forceful and true; but

[1] I am indebted for this and some other thoughts in this paragraph to Canon D. Macleane.

if He did not, then we must not only re-state our Christian belief, but we must re-establish it.

Once more, Bishop Wordsworth of Salisbury pointed out the significance of Galatians IV. 4: "When the fulness of the time came, God sent forth his Son, *made to be of a woman*" (γενόμενον not γεννήθεντα), which seems to exclude any human fatherhood. So far, then, from St. Paul being an adverse witness we may call him in on the side of the accepted belief, and claim that our case is as strong as can be reasonably asked, especially when the natural reserve and delicacy surrounding such a miracle are borne in mind.

A word may be said on the Buddha stories which have shaken some minds. These stories are so different from the Gospel accounts in detail, in motive and purpose that they need not trouble anyone. Edwin Arnold's *Light of Asia* is a dangerous book, and the danger is enhanced by the beauty of the poem. Those who only know that the Buddha lived five centuries before Christ may be shocked when they find so many Gospel incidents incorporated into the book; but those who know how common interpolation is in all Eastern literature will not be disturbed.

Again, Oriental myths are full of monstrous births of all sorts, but as far as my own reading has extended I know of no cases of true parthenogenesis. And so this section may be summed up in the words of Prof. Stanton: "The chief ground on which thoughtful Christian believers are ready to accept it (the miraculous birth) is that, believing in the personal, indissoluble union between God and man in Jesus Christ, the miraculous Birth of Jesus seems to them the only fitting accompaniment of this union, and, so to speak, the natural expression of it in the order of outward facts".[1]

Throughout this section I have employed the term "Virgin Birth" as it is popularly used; but speaking strictly there was nothing miraculous about the Birth of Jesus Christ. The miracle lay in the sinless *conception* on the part of the Blessed Virgin Mary through the overshadowing power of the Holy Spirit.

[1] *The Jewish and the Christian Messiah*, p. 376.

CHAPTER X.

CASTE.

THE position which caste occupies in the early stages of Hinduism is comparatively insignificant, but from the time when Manu wrote his Laws down to the present age, the place which it fills is of the greatest possible importance. It is the one and only bond that unites all Hindus together, holding, as they do, so many contradictory and heterogeneous beliefs. It is the point around which all Hinduism revolves. In the often quoted words of Bishop Sargent, "Caste is Hinduism, and Hinduism is caste". Going back to the very earliest ages when the Âryans invaded India caste divisions were unknown. These Âryans freely intermarried with the "natives" of India, ate with them, drank from the same wells, joined with them in their sacrifices and the sacrificial meals which necessarily accompanied the sacred rites (and doubtless the "sacred" cow was one of the animals offered), and so did just those things which are now anathema. Looking through the Vêdas we find no trace of caste, but the following passage is considered an adumbration of the system. The sage is describing the way in which the world was evolved from Purusha—the male and at the same time the supreme Deity—by the sacrifice of himself. He is cut into four parts, and thus, it is supposed, the four castes were produced.

"When they divided Purusha, how many portions did
they make?
What do they call his mouth, his arms? What do
they call his thighs and feet?
The Brâhman was his mouth, of both his arms was the
Râjanya made,
His thighs became the Vaisya, from his feet the Sûdra
was produced."

(*Rig Vêda*, X. 90, 11, 12.)

The absurdity of interpreting so mystic a passage in terms of the present rigid caste rules may be seen by quoting the next line:—

"The moon was gendered from his mind, and from
his eye the sun had birth".

Although there were no caste distinctions at first, the Âryans soon found it necessary to preserve their purity and sovereignty by abandoning all familiar intercourse with the natives. We find the fair-skinned settlers were soon at war with the brown Dasyus—probably the Drâvidians who had settled there many centuries earlier than themselves—and the black-skinned and savage aborigines.[1] The following stanza shows how Indra destroyed the godless races:—

[1] The "Dasyus" are enemies, and the "Dâsus" slaves. In spite of centuries of oppression they have not died out like the aborigines of Australia or the Maoris of New Zealand, but have flourished and been most prolific.

"Thou slewest with thy bow the wealthy Dasyu,
Alone, yet going with thy helpers, Indra!
Far from the floor of heaven in all directions,
The ancient riteless ones fled to destruction".
(*Rig Vêda*, I. 33, 34.)

Those, however, on whom the brunt of the fighting fell soon asserted themselves, and so the priestly Brâhmans had to allow the Kshatriyas to take rank after themselves. The "wealthy Dasyus" may be hated like the Jewish Shylock, but commerce and agriculture cannot be despised; and so to them were assigned the third and fourth places. The savage and foul aborigines, the Dâsus, were deemed unworthy of having any caste at all. Throughout the Divine Song caste is maintained, and Krishna in his argument claims to be the author of it. "The four castes," he says, "emanated from me, by the different distribution of energies and actions; know me to be the author of them, through the actionless and inexhaustible" (*Bhagavad Gîtâ*, IV. 13).

Let us now see how the Âryans—the forebears of the present Brâhmans—have established their supremacy and placed their yoke on all the inferior castes, and how they have degraded and ill-treated the outcastes. The institution of caste was, I repeat, at first unknown. But the Âryans, after they had conquered the natives, soon threw off all intercourse with them. To preserve their purity and to maintain their supremacy, they felt that they were forced to abandon all familiarity with the subject races. They would not allow them to bathe in the same streams with them, drink water from their wells, or take food with them. All social amenities were destroyed with a blow, and friendship was, of course, made an impossibility. They determined not to defile themselves even by touch with such foul carrion-eating people, and intermarriage was, above all, interdicted as the greatest of all possible crimes. But how, it will be asked, could such fetters be riveted on the necks of any nation? And how could the people be induced to asquiesce in and maintain for all these centuries an institution which fixed a yoke upon all their necks? By the simplest but most powerful expedient that the world knows—priestcraft. Once let the idea be established that some one person, or family or tribe is the infallible representative of God upon earth and all the rest follows simply and almost automatically. Let sceptics and agnostics set up any theories they like, but the great fact remains that all the people of the world, speaking broadly, are naturally religious; that there is no power on earth so strong as religion; and that the fight against religion is as foolish and hopeless a task as an effort to beat back the Niagara Falls with a broom. Caste developed at an amazing rate, largely because it also pandered to human pride—another factor common to all the world. None of us minds showing deference to "the quality," as our grandfathers used to say, so long as he can compel his inferiors to show deference to himself. By the time that Manu issued his Laws the caste system was fully established and bound as a willing burden on the backs of all the Indian people. It could, of course, only be maintained by religious sanctions, and its breach was to be punished with the direst penalties in this world and the next. To kick a Brâhman is a crime so dreadful that no torture, nor even death, could expiate it. The wicked one must pass through many painful births as a pig, or a worm on a dunghill, or even—to descend to still lower depths—as a Chândâla, or Pariah. We are told that "Those who lead bad lives (i.e. break caste rules) are born as dogs, pigs, or even as Chândâlas" (*Chhândogya Upan.*). There are now living in India upwards of fifty millions of wretched outcastes, whose ancestors have been trampled in the mire for centuries, and are not only held to be lower than the pigs that do the scavenging of the roads, but who have themselves accepted such degradation as part of the universal order. Their touch causes pollution, so that the Brâhman who has been hustled into a third-class railway carriage, or his son who has had to sit in school on the same bench with lower caste boys must bathe and dress in clean clothes before daring to taste food.

There are many people who admit that they know very little of the philosophy of India and have never heard of the Upanishads, who yet fancy that they know all about caste. As a matter of fact there are few things on which people have more erroneous notions than on this subject. There are several pitfalls into one of which they are almost sure to stumble. They will tell you that caste is dying out; and so show that they are either adopting a superficial view, or are confusing in their minds two very different things—caste among Hindus and caste among Christians. Or, they will assume that every Christian has totally and once for all given up caste, which, alas! is very far from being the case. Or, they will argue that if caste be left alone it will die out of its own accord both among Hindus and Christians. Or, lastly, they will maintain that caste is the same as social rank in England and America.

In the case of Brâhmans and other non-Christian Hindus it is true that caste in its grosser features is dying out and many high-caste Hindus educated in our western culture deplore the evils of caste, however woefully their deeds lag behind their words. The railways do to a certain extent tend to kill caste, but the *spirit* of caste is just as strong as ever. The present unrest in India is based on caste, because the Brâhman sees that he is losing the position of divine superiority which he has held for thousands of years. The Indian Government, working on its boasted lines of religious neutrality, cleverly hiding the light of Christianity under a bushel, and priding itself on its justice, is bound to appoint a certain small number of Muhammadans and Christians to civil posts where "twice-born" Brâhmans have to serve under them. Such action, so contrary to all their hereditary instincts and so degrading to all their ingrained assumptions of divine right, they resent most bitterly in the depths of their hearts. If we could compel the Pope of Rome to serve as a "Captain" under "General" Booth in the Salvation Army, we should soon find what a hornet's nest we had stirred up among the Roman Catholics. There is probably no problem on earth so difficult to solve as the race-problem; and caste is a particularly thorny branch of that thorny subject. It is idle to imagine that gentleness and politeness, however estimable such qualities are, can in themselves eradicate evils which reach down to the very depths of the human heart. Rose-water has its use, but we cannot conquer big battalions by spraying them with attar of roses. Let us think for a moment how caste and priestcraft have affected the history of India. The Brâhmans have completely isolated themselves from all the rest of the world by building round their country and themselves an exclusive wall greater and higher than any Wall of China, or even any Himâlayan range. They defeated Gautama and drove out the Buddhists, while assimilating much of that great reformer's teaching. Again, when assailed by the Muhammadans with the sword in one hand and the Quran in the other, they met them unarmed, save for their priestly panoply, and virtually reduced their conquerors to impotence. The Syrian Christians, and later, the Roman Catholics and Lutherans, found caste too strong for them, and yielded to it. Our own branch of the Catholic Church has made but a half-hearted resistance to caste and has weakened itself by permitting an intermingling of two opposite forces, the one tending to disintegration, and the other to union in the Fatherhood of God and the brotherhood of man. When we consider the Hindus as a nation we see what a hard task the Indian Government has before it, especially as it is so nervous about its own Christianity when dealing with the race-problem. And when we look at the Christian converts of our church we see all round the weakness that has resulted from failing to adopt a strong and decisive policy from the outset. A want of faith always leads to weakness and timidity, and these again result in a false policy pointing the road to ruin.

Passing on now to discuss this question of caste among Christians it must be owned that striking as has been the success of Christian missions—alas! that our church should take the lowest place—it must be admitted that this great success has been nullified and vitiated to a great extent by the admission of caste into Christianity.[1] Bishop Mylne rightly says that "Caste is the deadliest enemy with which the Gospel must grapple in India". When so many people, like ostriches with their heads in the sand, are vainly comforting themselves with the idea that caste will die out of its own accord, if left alone, it is well to emphasize such a remark. Weeds do not die out of their own accord, but leave seeds by the hundred and thousand behind them. Drunkards with weakened will and

[1] Those who wish for further information are referred to the chapter on this head in my *South Indian Missions* (S.P.G.).

craving thirst do not reform themselves of their own accord. It is caste that is the greatest stumbling-block to the reception of baptism by the Brâhmans and others who call themselves high caste. They themselves admit that they would become Christians were it not for caste. What this rupture of the caste bond means it is difficult for a Christian in England to conceive. No words of mine can be so forcible as those of Bishop Mylne, which I venture to quote:—

"One can imagine oneself cut off at a stroke from every one who has ever been dear to him, divorced from husband or wife, a stranger to the children of his bosom, homeless, impoverished, despised, having none to recognize or eat with him. But these, after all, are externals, and might leave the soul unashamed. What no European can picture is that this should come on him from without from the breach of a ceremonial prohibition, and that he should be conscious from within that it formed but the outward embodiment of an inward, ineradicable defilement which had cankered him body and soul; that he had not only forfeited his all as far as this world is concerned, but that he, in his innermost being, was a horror of loathsome pollution to God, to man, to himself; that there had come on him, in one fell swoop, every temporal and eternal anathema by which a human being can be blasted; that there was left out of the shipwreck of his all no plank, no broken piece of the ship, by which to escape to land; nay that there remained no friendly land to which escape might be made."[1]

Every word of this description is true, though I regret that I cannot follow the Bishop when he treats caste as a social system based, in his favourite method, on the doctrine of Pantheism. Caste has been so long tolerated because the social aspect has been emphasized to the exclusion of the religious (though not in the passage just quoted) that many people, including even missionaries, are apt to look upon it as a mere social evil.[2]

People who are oppressed and degraded, who are bound down by the thraldom of priestcraft and denied the most elemental rights of freemen, take refuge in the substitution of groups for individuals, for collective thought rather than individual opinion. All child-races talk in proverbs—the hereditary wisdom of the nation—and the custom of the caste becomes the law of life. If one sheep instead of crossing the bridge leaps over the parapet, every sheep in the flock does the same. It is not Pantheism, but awe in the presence of gods embodied in Brâhmanic form, and pride, which prompts the Brâhman to gather up his garments lest they should be defiled by the touch or presence of a carrion-eating inferior, and it is this that is the basis of caste. And to maintain the rigidity of such barriers

[1] *Hinduism as a Social System*, by Bishop Mylne, p. 13.

[2] Even when looked at as a social evil, it has been described as "The most disastrous and blighting of human institutions" (*Ancient Law*, by Sir H. S. Maine).

all the penalties of earth, and all the imagined tortures of hell, have been called into play and become part of the hereditary joint conviction of the caste community. Missionaries, especially in South India, see many illustrations of the power of caste. Many a wife and mother has thrown herself down the garden well because husband or son has brought irretrievable disgrace upon her, not so much by his belief in the Christian religion, as by breaking caste through the ceremony of the poured water. "What have I done to you," sobbed a widow, and mother of an only son, as she lay prone at my feet, begging me not to baptize him, "that you should bring this disgrace on me and my family?" The youth was of the thief caste, and though it is no disgrace to live by stealing, it is the greatest disgrace conceivable to break away from caste by baptism. The disgrace here is not merely social, but, as the Bishop says, one that cankers both body and soul with an ineradicable defilement.

But the majority of the present converts to Christianity do not belong to the Brâhman or other high castes. They are taken from the lower strata and rise rather than fall by becoming Christians. They have for the most part come over in masses, because their other caste people have done so, and hence they are unwilling when giving up their idols to abandon their position of supposed superiority to others lower than themselves. There is not a Pariah in the land, though called an "out-caste," that does not imagine that he is superior to some one else lower down in the caste scale, and he will fight to the last drop of blood in his veins to retain that position.

But the commonest excuse of all is that caste corresponds with social rank in Europe and America. Even missionaries who have not been brought into close conflict with this deadly evil, or who have not lived in South India, the strongest citadel of caste, sometimes adopt this fallacy, and it is to this fallacy that much of the weakness of Christianity in India is due in the case of our own Church, and still more among the Lutherans, and among the Roman Catholics. This was the fatal mistake which was made by, and which we have inherited from, the Lutheran missionaries of Germany three centuries ago, when the distinction between nobles and commoners was far more strongly marked than in the present democratic age. Caste is essentially a different thing from social rank, for the former is a birth-distinction, and has nothing to do with money, rank, education, or anything else in the world except birth. A man can no more change his caste than a sheep can change itself into a cow, or a man can change his sex. If a Pariah passed first in the Indian Civil Service examination, and became Chief Justice of the High Court, his touch would still defile the most ignorant and poverty-stricken Brâhman in the land. The latter would die a hundred deaths by torture rather than marry his daughter. To prove my case it will suffice to call in as witness the Rev. Nehemiah Goreh, a Brâhman of the Brâhmans, who as a scholar, a convert, and a controversialist knew

Hinduism as few people have known it through and through.

"A friend once read Goreh the speech of some English celebrity, in which it was stated that the missionaries made a great mistake in making their converts give up caste. The English themselves had caste, it was said, for the squire would not eat with his coachman.

"Goreh, disgusted with such ignorance, said: 'That man is talking nonsense. He does not know what he is saying; caste in India is this. We Brâhmans think we are gods, and therefore, none but our fellow Brâhmans who are gods too must come and touch us. We do not mind how ignorant or how poor a man is: if he be Brâhman we can dine with him. But this is not English caste. If the squire's coachman became a moneyed man and pushed his way in the world, the squire would not object to dining at the same table."

Once, when there was a controversy about the recognition or not of caste in South India, he took up the negative side very warmly, and said, "Christianity with caste would be no Christianity at all".[1]

It must be acknowledged that there is a race-problem in other parts of the world beside India. There it is more of a social than a religious question. But

[1] The present writer once discussed in the *Indian Church Quarterly Review* the evils of caste in a paper entitled *Caste with Christianity*, and another missionary excused its existence in the Church on the ground that it only corresponds with social rank in England. See the *Life of Father Goreh*, p. 7.

wherever the question of colour comes in there is always a great difficulty. Put a white man and a coloured man together in the same room, and the difficulty will at once be *felt*, though the white man may be a spiritually-minded man most anxious to span the gulf between himself and the other man whom he fully recognizes as his brother. The race-problem is one of the greatest, if not the greatest problem, with which the Church now has to deal. The solution can only be found in the great doctrine of the Fatherhood of God and the brotherhood of man as revealed in the Incarnation. In caste we have not only the race-problem but also superimposed on it a religious problem of the most difficult kind.

The modern Brâhman, who scorns Christianity as a religion of Pariahs, will talk glibly enough of the Fatherhood of God and the brotherhood of man, but his words are mere sounding brass and a clanging cymbal, because unaccompanied by the love that seeketh not its own. In the heart of his heart it is far better to abandon life than to abandon caste. The Divine Song is still to the educated Hindu what the Psalms are to the Christian.

"Better to do the duty of one's caste,
Though bad and ill-performed, and fraught with evil,
Than undertake the business of another,
However good it be. For better far
Abandon life at once than not fulfil
One's own appointed work ; another's duty

Brings danger to the man who meddles with it.
Perfection is alone attained by him
Who swerves not from the business of his caste."

(*Bhagavad Gîtâ*, III. 35; XVIII. 47, 48.)

As regards Indian Christians, so long as they decline to abandon caste entirely they are reaching out one hand to Christianity and the other to Hinduism, and so at best are only half Christians. St. Paul wrote to the Judaizing Christians, "Ye are severed from Christ, ye who would be justified by the law; ye are fallen away from grace" (Gal. v. 4). These are strong words, but not one whit too strong to be applied to the caste-keeping Christians of South India. The Church there is like a branch half-severed from the parent tree. How can the sap of divine Grace freely flow, and how can the flower bloom or the fruit ripen into the Christ-like character, which is the full development of the Christ-like life? It is here that the Incarnation meets our needs if properly understood and grasped. The shoot must be entirely severed from the wild olive tree and grafted into the good tree. There stands the eternal Stock, the root of Jesse, the true Vine, the tree of Life; and into that tree all branches must be grafted, must drink in the divine sap, be beautified with divine blossoms and laden with divine fruit.

To the mind of all Indians—alas! that it should have to be said of Christians as well as Hindus—there is no bond stronger than caste. Not only is "blood thicker than water," but "the blood is the life". All of one caste are brothers and sisters who must live and die for one another. The honour of one warms the heart of all, the disgrace of one burns like a fiery brand into the heart of all. Respect must be paid to the higher, but the bitterest antagonism must be offered to all below who aspire to equality with them or infringe their rights and privileges. Caste is not the poor weak thing which we call "social rank"; it is a thousand-fold stronger, for to break caste is a disgrace deeper than any shame in this world, a curse which to the Hindu even death and the tortures of hell and numberless re-births can scarcely purge. Is there not something grand as well as terrible in all this? Cannot these communities be led to realize their common union in the Incarnate One? "He is the head of the body, the church" (Col. I. 18), and "as many of you as were baptized into Christ did put on Christ. There can be neither Jew nor Greek, there can be neither bond nor free, there can be no male and female," there can be no Brâhman and Pariah, "for ye all are one man in Christ Jesus" (Gal. III. 27, 28). All are very members in the body of the Son who have been regenerated in Holy Baptism. If we could only induce the Christians of India—clergy as well as laity—to realize fully the true brotherhood of man by the union in the one God-man, then caste would become an impossibility; and, instead of a poor stunted tree with barren branches, there would flourish a "tree of life bearing twelve crops of fruit, yielding its fruit every month" (Rev. XXII. 2, margin).

CHAPTER XI.

VISHNU, SIVA AND THEIR INCARNATIONS.

As soon as a missionary begins his work in India as a worker and not a mere student, he finds that he is confronted not so much with the philosophy of the Vêdânta as the worship of two distinct gods, Vishnu and Siva, together with their female counterparts. He also finds that he has two distinct principles to deal with, corresponding to the two gods, the Way of Faith (*Bhakti-mârga*), and the Way of Works (*Karma-mârga*). Speaking of the Hindus of the higher castes these two gods and their systems practically overshadow everything else. Glancing back at the Vêdic period we saw the sources from which the gods sprung. Broadly speaking, Brahmâ was the Creator, Vishnu, the sun-god, was the Preserver, and Rudra, the storm-god, became ultimately Siva the Destroyer. At one time all three gods took equal rank and dignity:—

"In those three Persons the one God was shown—
Each first in place, each last—not one alone;
Of Siva, Vishnu, Brahmâ, each may be
First, second, third among the blessed three".[1]

[1] *Kumâra-sambhava*, VII. 44 (Griffith).

Brahmâ came to be looked upon under two aspects—as Prajâpathi, "the Lord of creatures, who offered himself as a sacrifice for the gods"; [1] and also as the first manifestation of the supreme Brahma of the Vêdânta. Between the Vêdic and the latter period, there was a tendency towards monotheism, while in the earlier Upanishads the phenomenal world continued to possess real existence. *Mâyâ* was an invention of a comparatively recent period. It was unknown till after the time of Buddha in the sixth century B.C. Then we come to the full-blown system of the Vêdânta, in which we have bare Existence, and for the rest nothing but Illusion. Now the idea of the Triad, in which the three letters AUM in the sacred syllable are supposed mystically to symbolize the Tri-mûrtti, has for all practical purposes passed out of notice. It is said that there is only one temple in all India, near Ajmîr, where Brahmâ is worshipped as God. Then Vishnu and Siva become rivals.

Taking Siva first, we often find him described as the "great god" (*mahâ dêva*), and his wife Kâli, or Durgâ, the "great goddess" (*mahâ dêvî*). Their symbols, the *linga* and the *yoni*, typify the male and female principles, and in their honour innumerable temples are found all over India. So that from the point of view of creation these two are of far greater importance than Brahmâ and his wife Sarasvati. Siva is called "the Blessed One," and is often identified

[1] *Tândya-brâhmana.* This sacrifice is sometimes attributed to Vishnu.

with Îsvara, the Lord. He is, however, chiefly the dissolver of the universe, the stern and terrible destroyer (Bhairava), but even in this capacity he is not equal in malignancy to the cruel goddess Kâli who is always thirsting for, and rejoicing in, human blood. In another aspect he is known as a rollicking libertine and shameless debauchee—so different from his other aspects—dancing with his wife and surrounded by a troop of buffoons. It is under this aspect that he and his wife are worshipped by the Tântrikas, as will be shown below. The marks by which Saivites are recognized—often erroneously called caste marks—are three lines drawn in ashes (*vibûti*) across the forehead, breast and arms. Another common mark is a black spot just above the nose which is supposed to be the god's third, or spiritual, eye. His son, variously known as Ganapati, Ganêsa, and Pillaiyar (the child), is to be seen with his grotesque elephant head in almost every village, and under innumerable wayside trees; and the son seems to be far more popular than the father. Though the symbols of Siva are to be found everywhere, the number of people who choose Siva himself as their particular divinity is comparatively small. He is so stern, ascetic, and cruel a god that he cannot compete with his great rival Vishnu.

Two observations must now be made which will detain us only for a moment. The first is that modern Hinduism among the higher castes, though, of course, associated with the philosophy of the Upanishads, and looking upon knowledge (*gnâna*) as the means of liberation, adds thereto two other methods. The stern Saivism adopts, as we have seen, the "Way of Works," that is penance, austerities, self-mutilation and so forth; while the gentler sect of Vaishnavism insists on *bhakti*, the "Way of Faith," as the means of personal attachment to God. The second point is that Saivism knows nothing of "incarnations," such as are attributed to Vishnu, though certain manifestations of Siva are sometimes called incarnations. Vîrabhadra, e.g., was formed from Siva's mouth for the purpose of taking vengeance on a sage who had omitted to invite Siva and Durgâ to a sacrifice with the other gods. He is a monstrous, savage creature with a thousand heads, eyes, and feet. Other manifestations of a similar kind, and all of a terrible form, are also known. Durgâ, too, takes all sorts of shapes to slaughter demons, but these are in no sense incarnations. What are known as the incarnations of Vishnu are, from the point of view of this essay, of far greater interest than anything that can be found in the corresponding devotion to Siva.

Vishnu (perhaps from *vis*, to pervade) diffuses light and life, and infuses his essence into various creatures, such as rivers, trees, animals, and human beings, and he is chiefly known by these "incarnations". His sect are recognized by the mark of his foot on the forehead. A white line rises from the bridge of the nose, and two other red or yellow lines are painted, one on each side, forming together a trident-shaped symbol. Men naturally turn from the austerity of

Buddha and the cruelty of Siva to the intensely human life of Vishnu's chief incarnation. Krishna, in spite of—perhaps it would be more correct to say, in consequence of—his intense wickedness, touches men's hearts. The Brâhmans were cunning enough, in their contest with Buddha, to see the importance of creating a popular and personal god who would appeal to men with their human affections and human passions.

It has already been noted that the word "incarnation" as applied to Vishnu is very different from the Christian use of the word as applied to our Blessed Saviour. The word *avatâra* simply means "descent," and the descents of Vishnu were only temporary. In one case only—that of Krishna—the incarnation is said to be a full human one, and in the others it is either a part of the essence that is supposed to be infused into men, like Râma, or else a still smaller part into an animal. At the best such an incarnation savours more of Docetism than of a true incarnation. The Church's doctrine of the Incarnation of Jesus Christ is that the Person of the Son of God existed from all eternity, that at His birth no new Person came into being and He who was the eternal Son "took man's nature in the womb of the Blessed Virgin, of her substance, so that two whole and perfect natures, that is to say the Godhead and the manhood, were joined together in one Person, never to be divided, whereof is one Christ, very God and very man" (*Article* 11). Hence, by what is called the "hypostatic union," two natures were inseparably and for ever united in one single hypostasis, or personal Self. There is nothing to correspond with this in the descent of Vishnu or Krishna, still less in any other so-called incarnation in Hinduism. For convenience' sake we may still continue to speak of Hindu incarnations, but we cannot admit that Krishna, according to Hinduism, is incarnate as Jesus Christ is. According to the Vêdântic teaching the supreme Self, the Brahma, by association with Illusion manifests Itself in all living things "from Brahmâ to a tuft of grass". Thus all the gods, Krishna, men, animals and plants are incarnations. The only difference between a god incarnate, like Krishna, and an ordinary man is that the former possesses the true knowledge (*gnâna*), by which he understands that "There is but One, no second" (*Êkam êva advitîyam*), and that all mundane existences are an illusion; whereas the latter can only test all these things by the evidence of his senses, which are themselves illusory.

There are ten descents of Vishnu which may now be described. One of the characteristics of Hinduism is that it has always been ready to absorb into its own system existing or opposing cults, so as to get rid of the opposition. This is certainly the case with the incarnation of Buddha. In other cases this is very likely to have been the case. They found tribes worshipping fish, boars, lions and so on, so they swallowed up their cults into their own religion. There were also legends which had been handed down for centuries, and it was found useful to incorporate them. The first three incarnations carry us back to the Flood.[1]

1. The Fish (*Matsya*). Here we have the story of Noah told in Indian language. Manu, not the law-giver of that name, but the progenitor of the human race, had gained the favour of Brahma by his austerities while all the rest of the world was sunk in sin. He was warned of the coming deluge, was ordered to build an ark, and to take the seven Rishis (holy sages), with various other creatures, on board. Vishnu assuming the form of a fish, when the flood rose, towed the ship by means of a cable attached to a horn on his head, and safely secured it to a lofty hill.

2. The Tortoise (*Kûrma*). The gods desired to churn the sea of milk to gain many precious things lost in the Flood. So Vishnu, as a tortoise, lay on his back at the bottom of the ocean, and became the pivot on which revolved the mighty mountain which the gods used as a pestle, the king of the snakes being coiled round it to serve as a rope. When the gods pulled alternately at each end of their rope, the sea became churned, and nectar, producing immortality (*amrita*) and many other valuable things were yielded up.

3. The Boar (*Varâha*). A demon had carried off the earth to the bottom of the sea, whereupon Vishnu took the form of a boar, waged war with the demon for a thousand years, slew him and then heaved up the earth on his tusks.

[1] See *Hinduism*, by Sir Monier Williams (S.P.C.K.).

4. The Man-lion (*Nara-sinha*). Another demon had gained as a boon from Brahmâ immunity from death. He first got dominion over the three worlds, heaven, earth, and the infernal regions (*pâtâla*), then he appropriated the sacrifices of the gods, and lastly tried to kill his own son for worshipping Vishnu. On this the latter assumed the form of a man-lion, and tore him in pieces.

5. The Dwarf (*Vâmana*). King Bali—and *bali* means sacrifice—had performed a sacrifice of such marvellous power that he had got the sovereignty over the three worlds, and so superseded even the great god Indra. Vishnu then went to the king as a dwarf, and begged him to grant him as much land as he could stride over in three steps. On gaining his request he strode over heaven and earth, and left Bali only the lower regions. Vishnu was originally the sun-god, and this may have given rise to the idea of his striding over the earth.

6. Râma with the axe (*Parasu-Râma*). Now we come into the region of history and hero-worship. The Brâhmans had great difficulty in maintaining their supremacy over the other castes, especially the Kshatriyas, or warriors. Supremacy can only be maintained by one of two means, the power of the sword, and the power of priestcraft. Nowadays we say that "the pen is mightier than the sword," but amongst illiterate people there is no power more potent than priestcraft. The Kshatriyas, as the conquerors of the country, arrogantly claimed the first rank as superiors of the Brâhman priests, and so Vishnu took the form

of Râma with the axe, and repeatedly slaughtered the audacious Kshatriyas. It may be remarked in passing that all the trouble in India now rises from the same idea. However tolerant of caste the British Government may be, the Brâhmans, a small but educated class, know that they cannot take the first rank so long as the English remain in the country.

7. Râma. He is generally called Râma-chandra, the moon-like, or gentle Râma. Vishnu infused half his essence into him. He is India's type of a brave soldier, while Sîtâ, his wife, is her type of chaste womanhood. The Râmâyana is the epic poem which describes the adventures of Râma when he led an expedition to Ceylon to recover his wife Sîtâ, who had been carried off by the tyrant Râvana. Râma is one of the finest characters in India, and so the modern reformers adopted his name in the formation of their sects.

8. Krishna, "the dark god". Vishnu assumed this incarnation to destroy the tyrant Kansa. As this is the only complete incarnation of Vishnu, and as Krishna is the most popular god in India, his history will be given more fully below.

9. Buddha. According to the Hindus Vishnu adopted this incarnation so as to delude demons and wicked men into bringing the Vêdas and caste rules into contempt, and so lead to their own destruction. Instead of this inadequate reason, perhaps we may be excused if we give a reason of our own. Sâkya Muni had challenged the empty ritual of the Brâhmans; he

had condemned the cruelty of innumerable sacrifices, and had denounced the evils of caste. They resorted to the sword and persecution to crush this sceptical heretic. They had to meet his arguments by reasoning of their own, through which the whole character of Hinduism became revolutionized. Next, they evolved the idea of the human, pleasure-loving, and licentious Krishna to combat the austerities and personal influence of the enlightened reformer, who by his earnestness and sincerity had attracted to himself thousands of enthusiastic followers. And then, as a last measure, they conciliated his adherents and absorbed his system by making Buddha one of the incarnations of their own god. The cleverness which the Brâhmans displayed in overcoming the greatest and most powerful antagonist that Hinduism has ever had to confront is amazing. The Muhammadans came later with the sword in one hand and the Quran in the other. And now there is a stronger opponent than either of these to be faced; and the Brâhmans would be only too thankful to effect a compromise, or place Christ on a pedestal with Buddha and Krishna.

10. Kalki. This incarnation has still to appear at the end of the fourth, or iron age (*kali yuga*), when the world has become so utterly wicked that it will have to be destroyed to make way for the age of truth (*satya yuga*).

Now let us return to Krishna. One of the commonest things that an Indian missionary hears is that "Krishna is the same as Christ". So we must examine the life and history of this popular god more fully. He appears in two entirely different aspects—the first a more or less noble one, the second an utterly bad one. It will not be necessary to write at length about the former, because so much has already been said of his teaching in the Divine Song. We see him there as an incarnation who has come to the earth at a time of great peril and wickedness to set the world right. It is true that he advocates the slaughter of Arjuna's relatives, but he speaks as a philosopher expounding the nature of Brahma, and showing the identity of man's soul with that of the Supreme. Still we cannot shut our eyes to the other picture of his character. In this book an endeavour has been made to expound the tenets of Hinduism as fairly as possible, and without anything of the nature of abuse; but if we ignore the other side of Hinduism and its obscene literature we expose ourselves to a great danger. Fifty years ago missionaries were frequently blamed for their gross attacks on Hinduism; but now there is a risk of running into the opposite extreme. We are so careful not to hurt anyone's susceptibilities, and so ready to lay hold of all that is good in other religious systems, that the Hindus are beginning to exclaim, "The two religions are the same; there is nothing to be found in Christ which has not got its counterpart in Krishna".

For the evidence concerning the life of Krishna we must look to the Vishnu and Bhagavata Purânas. At the time when the antagonism between the sects of

Vishnu and Siva became acute, the Purânas were written to exalt one deity over the other; and these two Purânas deal chiefly with the legends of Krishna. Kansa had taken the throne of Mathurâ from Vasudêva, the lawful king, and as he had been warned that a son of Vesudêva and his wife Dêvakî would kill him, he had them fettered and immured in a fortress. When, however, the child was born, the fetters fell off, and Vasudêva fled across the Jumna with his son and placed him in the house of a cowherd, Nanda, whose wife had just given birth to a daughter. Whether this story of the changeling is due to a reminiscence of Herod and the holy innocents, or whether it was invented by the Brâhmans to get over the difficulty of Krishna not being a Brâhman by caste, one can say nothing definite. As a plain historical fact Krishna was an Indian prince of the warrior caste who fought on the side of the Pandavs against the Kauravs, as described in the Mahâbhârata. According to the Purânas he was noted in his childhood for disobedience to his mother, for lying and stealing, and every other form of childish wickedness. As a boy he stole the butter of the *gopis* or milkmaids, and lied about it. When he had grown up he took Râdhâ the wife of Ayanagosha, and when the husband was on the point of catching them in their adultery, he suddenly changed himself into the figure of Kâli so that Râdhâ might appear to be engaged in an act of worship. If there is one thing more than another that offends all Hindus in these days it is cow-killing. Yet we read of

Krishna killing a bull that had attacked him. He took the clothes of the *gopis* while bathing, and compelled them to come to him in their nude state to beg him to give them back. This incident forms one of the commonest pictures that may be seen in the houses of his modern followers. Cheap coloured prints of it are imported from Europe by thousands to adorn the walls of their houses. Besides eight queens, he is said to have had 16,100 wives, and 180,000 sons; but Hindus always delight to deal in figures of astronomical vastness. Many of his sons he slew in mad passion. Finally he was accidentally shot by a Bhîl hunter, and so abandoned the three *gunas*, or qualities.

His dancing and adultery with the *gopis* is called *lîlâ*, or sport, by the Hindus and his conduct is justified on the plea that "The mighty are not to be blamed". But as Bishop Caldwell remarked, "The stories related of Krishna's life do more than anything else to destroy the morals and corrupt the imagination of the Hindu youth". In the Mahâbhârata Krishna justified lying in the following circumstances: "On an occasion of marriage, or of enjoying a woman, or when life is in danger, or when one's entire property is about to be taken away, or for the sake of a Brâhman, falsehood may be uttered. These five kinds of falsehoods have been declared sinless." In the *Bhagavad Gîtâ* Krishna says;—

"Whensoever, O descendant of Bhârata, piety languishes, and impiety is in the ascendant, I create myself. I am born age after age, for the protection of the good, for the destruction of evildoers and the establishment of piety" (IV. 7, 8).

It was then certainly the duty of this Krishna to destroy the vile Krishna of the Purânas. However much the Hindus may try to allegorize away the legends of Krishna's life, there is no doubt that the great mass of his followers gloat over these obscene stories and suffer the consequent demoralization. To mention the all-holy Jesus in the same breath as this monster of wickedness would be a profanity.

There is a sect of the followers of Krishna, founded by Vallabha in the sixteenth century, who call themselves his incarnations, and who claim to act as he did. It is declared that the best way to propitiate Krishna is for the disciples to minister to the carnal desires of these so-styled Mahârâjas.

While on this painful subject I must refer to the Tantras. The manifestations of Siva are, I repeat, unimportant; but those of his wife, Kâli, or Durgâ, call for notice. Each god has his *sakti*, that is his female energy, or active power, in all the operations of creation, preservation and destruction. As Siva was supposed to embrace within himself all the attributes of the gods, so also his wife was held to represent all their female manifestations, and to absorb into herself all their functions. So also, just as the Purânas were written to glorify Vishnu and his "descents," so the Tantras were composed to describe the manifestations of Siva and his *sakti*. The system is called Tântrism, or Sâktism, on this account, and is so licentious that it must be dismissed as briefly as possible. The *sakti* is the left side of Siva, and so the Sâktis are known as " left-hand worshippers ". The goddess Durgâ has two distinct functions, the cultivation of the intercourse between the sexes, and the attainment of magical powers ; and so it may be readily imagined that the results of Sâktism are degrading in the extreme. Sir William Hunter describes the system as " an organized fivefold ritual of incantation, lust, gluttony, drunkenness and blood ". One strange thing about these debaucheries is that even the rules of caste—the strongest bonds that Hinduism knows—are relaxed. So long as the carnal love meetings last, there is indiscriminate association in unbridled lust of men and women irrespective of caste restrictions or marriage relations—and all this under the sanction of religion ! I must apologize to my readers for speaking of such things, but the dark side of Hinduism cannot be passed over entirely.

There is a popular belief among the Hindus that when the present " iron age " is over, the " true age " will commence, and then will appear the tenth *avatâr* of Vishnu riding a white horse with a drawn sword in his hand. What the Vishnu Purâna actually states is that, " when the close of the Kali age shall be nigh, a portion of that divine Being who exists of his own spiritual nature in the character of Brahma . . . shall descend upon earth. . . . By his irresistible might he will destroy the Mhlechchhas (i.e. unclean out-castes) and thieves, and all whose minds are devoted to iniquity. He will then re-establish righteousness upon earth." This popular belief of the Hindus recalls to our minds the vision which St. John saw when the heaven was opened :—

"Behold a white horse, and he that sat thereon, called Faithful and True; and in righteousness he doth judge and make war . . . His name is called the Word of GOD. . . . Out of his mouth proceedeth a sharp sword . . . and he hath on his garment and on his thigh a name written, KING OF KINGS, AND LORD OF LORDS!" (Rev. XIX. 11 ff.).

This tenth *avatâr* of Vishnu faintly adumbrates an idea which has never found a permanent home in Hinduism; but even as an adumbration it may be welcomed in the hopes that India will soon embrace in this "true age" the Incarnation of the Lord Jesus Christ.

CHAPTER XII.

SOME PHASES OF MODERN HINDUISM.

WHEN I was an undergraduate at Cambridge I had to study the dynamics of a particle. It was necessary to give a great deal of thought to calculate the flight of projectiles with reference to their muzzle velocities, their trajectories, the distance carried and so forth.

After mastering these difficulties I was disgusted to read a footnote at the end of the text-book to the effect that these calculations were valueless because of varying wind pressures. After studying Hinduism, and also spending my life as a missionary dealing with the actual life and belief of Indians, I feel that Hinduism —the Hinduism of the great mass of the people whom one meets in the bazars, the villages and even in the schools and Colleges—is one thing in the books and quite another in the outer world. Nice mathematical calculations are at the back of the gunner's practice; but the divergence between the theory and the practice as regards the knowledge of Hinduism is much wider and much more complicated, nay, the two move for the most part on entirely different planes. It is necessary to insist on this because one so constantly sees statements to the effect that the mass of the Indian people are imbued with the higher Hinduism.

One writer represents every villager as saturated with the teaching of the Vêdânta and singing songs from the two great Epics while at his work. Another tells us, as we have seen above, that "Hinduism in every stage is at the core pantheistic," whereas it is extremely doubtful if Hinduism is in any stage at all pantheistic in the ordinary sense of that word. Others would have us believe that there are as many Hindus in India who study the "Divine Song" as there are Christians in the world who study and love the Bible. Such exaggerations, which no practical missionary would be guilty of, do harm because they mislead readers who rely on such authors as authorities. The vast majority of the hundred millions of Hindus know nothing whatever either of the Upanishads or of the *Bhagavad Gîtâ*—or, if they do know of them, they do not know them as systems seriously affecting their lives or religious observances. Their religion may be tinged by the Vêdânta almost unconsciously, just as our own conceptions about heaven, hell, the war of angels, etc., are tinged by Milton. The illiterate peasants of India know just as much about the *Bhagavad Gîtâ* as our own English peasants know about the *Paradise Lost.*

The Brâhmans of India number about seven per cent of the Hindus. The degraded out-castes, who know even less of the Upanishads than they do of the Divine Song, number about twenty-six per cent, and of the remaining sixty-seven per cent of non-Brâhmans and Sûdras, by far the greater proportion are incapable of signing their own names, and know nothing of the deep mysteries with which these pages have treated as formative or dominant forces in their religious lives. I was once asked to give a lecture in the S.P.G. College, Trichinopoly, which with the neighbouring town of Srîrangam, one of the "sacred" places of all India, is a centre of both Vaishnavism and Saivism, as well as the cradle of the great reformer Râmânuja and the poet Tâyumânavar. In this College there are about two-hundred-and-fifty Brâhman and high-caste lecturers and students. The subject which I chose was the *Advaita* system (One-without-a-second) of the Vêdânta, but I was dissuaded from adopting it by one of the Hindu lecturers, because he assured me that scarcely any of those present would understand my subject. And what then shall we say of the villages—and India is a land of innumerable villages? It will be urged that we must study the religion of the leaders and of the learned classes. True, but we must remember that caste has dug a vast gulf between the Brâhmans and Sûdras, and still another gulf between the Sûdras and the out-castes. Though it is common to speak about "the people of India," India is anything but a homogeneous country. Each village and each caste in that village has its own headmen, but of leaders in the wider sense India has none. The Brâhmans, who are the educated class, are the last people to lead or influence the Pariahs.

The higher and lower Hinduism are inextricably mixed, each modifying and being modified by the other, but they rest on entirely different bases. The non-Âryan cults, dating back to an unknown past long anterior to the Âryan invasion, still survive in all their vigour in spite of Brâhmanism and Vêdântism. Hence there are innumerable forms of religion from the cults of Vishnu and Siva down to the gross polytheism of the idolater, cruel and horrible sacrifices, and grotesque ceremonies of the animist and the devil-propitiator. The higher and lower Hinduism are not only different in their outward expression, but in their very essence. The physician must study chemistry, and the surgeon anatomy, or their patients will die under their hands; but a study of higher Hinduism will yield no guidance to the knowledge of the religious practices of the lower. The Âryan and the Drâvidian are like two different trees, which are planted side by side, and whose branches are closely intermingled, but which possess separate roots.[1] I desire to emphasize this view, because it will not be found in the ordinary text-books on Hinduism. Being in opposition to the opinions of these authorities, I can only plead *experto crede* and adduce my proofs. The practical work of a missionary has convinced me of the truth of what I assert; and, indeed, without the recognition of this difference I do not see how we are to escape from a hopeless labyrinth of inconsistencies and contradictions. Nothing can

[1] What is called the "marriage" of two different trees in this way may be seen in almost every village of South India.

possibly reconcile the monism of the Vêdânta, wherein thought has been pushed to its utmost limit to show that there is nothing in the world save the bare existence of Brahma, with the polytheism of the Drâvidians who worship three hundred millions of gods and goddesses in innumerable different ways, with the cults of animists, or, with the propitiation of so-called devil-worshippers.

Let me then try, however inadequately, to show what the religion of the great mass of people called Hindus really is, apart from the higher Hinduism. Beginning with those who are most influenced by the latter, and descending the scale, we find a strange medley of Saivism and Vaishnavism, *karma* and transmigration, of *bhakti* and animism, of devotion of the phallic emblem, the idolatrous worship of all manner of gods and goddesses, of sacred animals, snakes and certain trees, including the cults of endless village deities, the propitiation of devils, fetichism, magic and fatalism. Coupled with the belief of innumerable gods and goddesses (chiefly the latter), of greater or less power, and of devils and evil spirits of greater or less malignancy, there is an underlying notion of some shadowy God, who in some unknown mysterious way presides over all. "God's in His heaven, all's right with the world," sings Browning: "God's in His heaven, we may safely ignore Him," reflects the Hindu, harassed with many cruel devils and vindictive goddesses. Together with this vague idea of God there is the desire for forgiveness expressed in pilgrimages and bathings, and still more marked by the sacrifice of certain animals—a thing abhorrent to the orthodox Hindu. Binding all these people with their various beliefs, rites and ceremonies, in one bond common to them all, is caste, the most adamantine of all bonds, and yet—for India is a veritable jungle of paradoxes—the greatest disintegrating factor in the world.

Shrines grow up on the roadside as readily as trees; and a pat of mud on the bank of a river may at any moment be shaped into a *linga* (the phallic emblem), and worshipped as divine by the traveller on his journey. One may see an ant-hill, whose hole is probably the abode of the sacred cobra, dusted with red ochre and lighted every night with a small lamp, made out of a broken potsherd and a bit of twisted cotton as wick, develop in a few months into a wayside shrine. I have seen the grave of a stone-digger, who died at his work, marked off from the surrounding rocks on the hillside, grow into a similar shrine. It has now a wall of rough stones round it, which will probably develop into a regular temple with a consecrated idol inside, and a priest—if the word may be allowed to pass—who will stir up the emotion of pilgrims, and stimulate their offerings, by relating some miraculous legend, or by displaying some thaumaturgic power. There are no "services" in ordinary temples, such as we Christians are accustomed to, though in the large temples of the orthodox Hindus various "priests" will perform *pûja* (worship) all day long with elaborate ritual and much music in the small, innermost shrine of the edifice. When all goes well with the lower class Hindu he does not trouble himself much about his gods and goddesses; but when epidemics break out and annual ceremonies are to be observed, then the Hindu shows that religion belongs to the very fibre of his life. He is not shy or ashamed of his religion, like an Englishman, but when sacrifices or other ceremonies are to be performed, then every man, woman and child in the village is eager to be present.

One other remark must be made before I come to my illustrations. Just as there is a wide border-land between the higher and lower Hinduism, so is there a border-land between Hinduism and Christianity which finds its expression in many strange ways. There are several societies, or *samâjes*, founded by such great reformers as Râm Mohun Roy and Kêshab Chander Sen, which have incorporated much of Christianity into their eclectic systems. Of these the Ârya *samâj* is the most flourishing. There are also the reformed sects, which have sprung up under the influence of Râmânuja's teaching, with differing creeds, preached by such men as Râmânand, Tulsi Dâs and Kabir Dâs. These sects have for the most part a theistic basis, and adopt *bhakti* (faith, devotion, piety) as the central feature, leading up to an affectionate attachment to a divine Personality, just as in Christianity. Then there is the Theosophic movement led by Mrs. Besant, a lady gifted with exceptional rhetorical power. Her system is a curious blend of the teaching of the old Rishis with her hereditary Christian faith, which though formally rejected continues to crop up in spite of herself. It is a weird medley of Christianity, English common sense and Indian science run mad. Most strenuous efforts are made to popularize this system by incorporating into it everything likely to please the Hindus; but though the cult professes to be based on the Vêdânta with *karma*, transmigration and the rest; and though the high priestess herself professes to remember her former birth; and though she has founded a College for Hindus at Benâres; yet the result is a pitiful failure. The orthodox Hindus naturally look askance, however much flattered they may feel, at this strange English lady, the wife of a clergyman, proclaiming the glories of their Rishis, but mixing up with her teaching such foreign ideas. All these eclectic systems are, of course, drawn from the higher Hinduism, but are really revolts from it. They need not detain us; but their resemblance to the Neo-platonism prevalent in the early days of the Church is certainly very remarkable. I will not repeat what I have said in another book;[1] but those who are interested in such matters will be struck by the remarkable historic parallel between the state of the Church in the second century under the Roman Empire and that of India at the present time under the British râj.

Many writers on India, as said above, after dealing with the Vêdântic philosophy and describing the worship of the two favourite gods Vishnu and Siva,

[1] *South Indian Missions*, p. 294 (S.P.G.).

seem to think that they have said enough and leave their readers to conclude, if they do not actually say so, that the religion of the common people is practically the same as that of the more or less educated and more or less high-caste men who live in the towns. A greater mistake could scarcely be made, for ninety per cent of the Hindus live in villages, a still greater percentage are illiterate, and their religion, as I shall now proceed to show, is not, strictly speaking, based on Hinduism at all, but on pre-Âryan practices and ceremonies. Its real basis is sacrifice, and so it is in closer touch with the polytheism of the Vêdas than with the mysticism of the Upanishads. The *pûjâris*, i.e. the men who perform the sacrifices and are masters of the ceremonies, are not Brâhmans or "priests" at all, but rather hereditary office-bearers who have learnt from their fathers the usual ritual of their caste and cult. Another important difference lies in the fact that the deities of the villages are almost invariably females instead of males as in Hinduism proper. It is true that these female deities are generally associated with a male guardian—generally Iyenâr in the Tamil country, with which I am best acquainted. The prevailing idea is that the supreme God is good and so may be disregarded; whereas the spirits are evil and will cause smallpox and cholera to break out, will kill their children, afflict their cattle, and ruin their crops. These bad spirits must therefore be propitiated with blood sacrifices, especially in times of epidemic disease and famine.

There is another point of interest which shows how the higher Hinduism has influenced the lower. It has already been shown how Buddha waged war against two great evils, namely, sacrifice and caste, and this went on during the last few centuries preceding the Incarnation. His influence and the new ideas about transmigration were sufficiently strong to banish all blood sacrifices from among the orthodox Hindus. Altars may still be seen in the old temples of Vishnu and Siva; but when I have asked Brâhmans for an explanation of the same, they have expressed horror at the idea of blood-shedding, but have never been able to account for the presence of these relics of an age long past. The lower classes, however, have always maintained their sacrifices from time immemorial. But when they slay their buffaloes, goats, pigs and cocks, etc., to appease the wrath of their goddesses, they generally keep the doors of the temple locked; or, if the deity be out in the open air, they envelop her figure in a shroud, lest she should see the victim being slain in her presence and to her honour. Inconsistency seldom troubles the mind of the Hindu, and so he makes no attempt to reconcile the two opposite ideas of horror and appeasement. And we English people love compromise so much ourselves that we cannot afford to throw stones at other people's glass-houses.

I will now briefly describe a few sacrificial ceremonies which have fallen within my own experience of thirty-one years in the Trichinopoly and Tinnevelly districts of South India. First of all, we must remember that the goddess herself may be represented by all sorts of different articles, such as a rude image of a female cut in stone, a brass or earthenware pot full of water, a rough unhewn block of stone, or a stick more or less carved. Cold weather visitors often take photographs of grotesque figures of horses, elephants, lions, giants and so forth, which they imagine to be gods; but fail to notice a rough bit of black and well-oiled stone projecting a few inches from the ground, which is the real goddess, while the monstrous figures are only guardians and night watchmen whose duty it is to keep off all the foul spirits with which the air is charged. Some goddesses are, however, quite elaborate figures. There is an idol in the Trichinopoly district consisting of a stone image of a woman, about two and a half feet high, with eight arms, and holding in her hands a knife, a shield, a bell, a devil's head, a drum, a three-pronged fork, a goad, and a piece of rope.

THE APPEASING OF A GODDESS.

About two miles from the mission house at Trichinopoly stands the temple of a goddess on the bank of a river, which has been dammed up for irrigation purposes. Her name is Kulumâi, "the lady of the dam". Every year, about the end of February, a great sacrifice is held to propitiate the wrath of this female deity. On the night before the festival a number of men and boys go to the temple and conduct in procession a representation of the goddess—who of course cannot be moved—in a quaint car, borne on four men's shoulders like a palanquin, with flaring torches and much noisy music, to the suburb of the town in which the mission house is situated. The din of the band and the blaze of the torches are kept up throughout the night till the sun dawns. Then the *pûjâri*, a coarse man of the Vellâla, or cultivator, caste wearing fantastic headgear, and wreathed with garlands of oleander, comes to conduct the day's sacrifices. The goddesses' own *pûjâri*, strange to say, has nothing to do with the day's work. By this time tens of thousands of the lower classes have poured into the town and swelled the ordinary population of over a hundred thousand inhabitants to an enormous crowd. From one to two thousand kids, which must be entirely black, are penned by the roadside, bleating piteously as if aware of the fate in store for them. The *pûjâri* mounts on the shoulders of two men in front of the representation of Kulumâi in her car, and then the heads of each family press round to offer each his kid to appease the anger of the goddess. A knife is slashed across the throat and the bleeding kid is held up to the *pûjâri*, who pretends to drink from the wound the victim's blood, and to revel on behalf of the goddess in the ghastly orgy. One kid after another is offered up, and all day long the sickening process continues. I have also seen the *pûjâri* take a silver bowl, holding a quart or more, fill it with the hot blood, and then drink it off, as if the goddess through him were greatly enjoying the horrible draught. By this means the deluded people think that they are protecting themselves, their families, their cattle, and their crops from all manner of injury and sickness. It need scarcely be said that in all such enormous crowds not one single Brâhman or orthodox Hindu will be found.

GUARDING THE BOUNDARIES.

Eleven miles from Trichinopoly there is another of these famous female deities, called Karumbâi, whose chief function is to ward off cholera. Of course it is of the utmost importance that cholera shall be kept out of the village, if possible; and so, instead of describing her usual sacrifice, I will relate the common sacrificial ceremonies observed to guard the village boundaries from the attacks of neighbouring spirits. After a week's offerings of fruit and rice, an earthen pot is specially prepared by similar offerings to the pot itself, and this becomes, as in the former case, the representation or temporary residence of the deity. Next, the *pûjâri* has a lamb sacrificed before him to make him fit to become possessed with the goddess during the ceremony; and a *kâpu*, or bangle, of thread dyed with turmeric is bound round his wrist to prevent any evil spirit from assailing him. He then carries off the pot to a booth in the middle of the village, accompanied with the usual band and the burning of incense and camphor, with offerings of coco-nuts, rice and fruit. On the last and great day of the ceremonies, a lamb is sacrificed by decapitation, and the blood is poured into another pot containing boiled rice. The *pûjâri*, now half frantic with the possession of the goddess, rushes off with the pot, the villagers running after him and yelling, till he comes to the boundary stone. After circling the stone thrice, he throws the pot backwards so that it shall fall on another stone placed there for the purpose, by means of which the mixed rice and blood may be scattered all round, and the evil spirits of other villages may not be able to trespass on the village thus protected.

A still more elaborate sacrifice, with many other strange and interesting ceremonies, has been described in detail in the *Nineteenth Century and After* of October, 1906.[1] These accounts show that the Drâvidian customs in the Telugu country are practically the same as those observed in the Tamil region.

A BUFFALO SACRIFICE.

"At a village called Turaiyûr near Trichinopoly a buffalo sacrifice is offered once in five or six years. Before the day of the festival is fixed, the chief men of the village go to the shrine, offer rice and fruits, etc., and ask the goddess whether they may perform the festival. If a lizard utters a chirp in a part of the temple fixed on beforehand, it is taken as a sign that permission is given and the festival is arranged. The buffaloes devoted for sacrifice are generally chosen, some time beforehand, by people who make vows in sickness or trouble, and then are allowed to roam

[1] *Village Deities in South India*, by Bishop Whitehead of Madras.

about the village at will. When they become troublesome, the people go and ask the deity to hold a sacrifice. The buffaloes are brought to the shrine on the appointed day, and killed by a man of the Kallar (thief) caste, who cuts off the head with a chopper. Nothing is done with the blood, but both head and carcase are thrown into a pit close by the shrine as soon as the animal is dead. The same pit is used at each festival, but it is cleared out for each occasion. When all the carcases have been put in, incense and camphor are burnt, coco-nut and fruits are offered on the edge of the pit, and then earth is thrown in, and the carcases are covered up. This takes place outside the temple walls, and during the sacrifice a curtain is drawn before the shrine, where the immovable stone image of the goddess is located; but, on the other hand, the metal image, used in processions, is taken out before the sacrifice begins, carried on a wooden lion, and placed on four stone pillars specially erected for the purpose outside the temple, about four or five yards from the place where the buffaloes are killed. No curtain is drawn before this image, but the sacrifice is performed in full view of the goddess. It is a curious little compromise between ancient custom and Brâhman prejudice."[1]

HUMAN SACRIFICE.

The Meriah sacrifice, in which a human being was the victim, has, of course, been suppressed by the

[1] Madras Museum, *Bulletin* V. No. 3, p. 170.

Indian Government, though it has been practised in secret till quite a recent time. A most interesting relic in the shape of a human sacrifice-post has lately been secured and presented to the Madras Museum.[1]

"The best known case," writes Mr. Frazer in *The Golden Bough*, "of human sacrifices systematically offered to ensure good crops is supplied by the Khonds or Khands, a Drâvidian race in Bengal and Madras. Our knowledge of them is derived from accounts written by British officers, who, forty or fifty years ago, were engaged in putting them down. The sacrifices were offered to the earth goddess, Tari Pennu or Bera Pennu, and were believed to ensure good crops, immunity from all diseases and accidents. In particular, they were considered necessary in the cultivation of turmeric, the Khonds arguing that the turmeric could not have a deep red colour without the shedding of blood. The victim, a Meriah, was acceptable to the goddess only if he had been purchased, or had been born a victim, that is the son of a victim father, or had been devoted as a child by his father or guardian."

HOOK-SWINGING.

Allied to such sacrifices is the practice of hook-swinging, which is not absolutely stopped, but is discouraged as much as possible by the Indian Government. In the districts in which I was myself engaged no hook-swinging has taken place of recent years, but

[1] *Ethnographic Notes in Southern India*, by Mr. E. Thurston, C.I.E., p. 510. The subject has been well treated in fiction by Mrs. Penny in her *Sacrifice*.

one or two have been held in the district of Madura between Trichinopoly and Tinnevelly. The following account was written in the eighteenth century by Sonnerat, and represents, in all the important items, what is still practised occasionally:—

"Those who imagine that they have received great benefits from Mariatale, or wish to obtain them, make a vow to suspend themselves in the air. This ceremony consists in passing two iron tenter-hooks, tied to the end of a very long lever, through the skin of the votary's back. This lever is placed at the top of a mast twenty feet high. As soon as the votary is hung on the hooks, they press the other end of the lever, and lift him up in the air. In this state they turn him round as often as he chooses. He commonly has a sword and shield in his hands, and makes the motions of a man fighting. He must appear cheerful, whatever pain he may feel: for, if tears escape him, he is driven from his caste, but this seldom happens. The votary who is to be hung up drinks some intoxicating liquor, which makes him almost insensible, and looks upon this dangerous preparation as a pastime. After turning him several times round, they take him off, and he is soon cured of his wounds. The quickness of the cure passes for a miracle in the eyes of the zealots of this goddess. The Brâhmans do not assist at this ceremony, which they despise. The worshippers of Mariatale are of the lowest caste." [1]

This remark about the Brâhmans is illuminative.

[1] *Ethnographic Notes*, p. 490.

The following quotation is also instructive as showing the motive which induces people to submit to such cruel and painful rites :—

"Quite recently the Governor of Madras was approached by a ryot (agriculturalist), on behalf of the community, with a request for permission to revive the practice of hook-swinging in a certain village of the Madura District. He represented, with all earnestness, that since this ceremony had been stopped, the rainfall had been deficient and the crops scanty; cholera had been prevalent; and in families where there were five or six children ten years ago, there were now only two or three." [1]

FIRE-WALKING.

One other ceremony, that of fire-walking, may now be described. A pit, varying in size from a few feet to a few yards, is dug to a depth of about a foot, and filled with lighted faggots and charcoal till the whole blazes up, and then settles down into a glowing mass of red-hot embers. Then men, women and even children, who have previously bathed and performed other religious ceremonies, walk across the glowing fire. As a rule they are none the worse for their walk, but on one or two occasions people have fallen on the fire and subsequently died from the effect of the burning. The object of walking is generally to fulfil some vow after sickness, or on the birth of a

[1] *Ethnographic Notes*, p. 498.

child long hoped for; and there is also the common idea of securing protection from damage to crops and cattle, etc. This ceremony like others of the kind is despised by Brâhmans, and left to Sûdras and the lowest castes. It must be remembered that the soles of the feet of the labouring classes are very thick; but this will not always account for the immunity of the fire-walkers. Bathing is an essential feature of the ceremony, and it is not improbable that the feet of the devotees are bathed, unknown to themselves, not with water but with the juice of the *Aloe indica*, called in Tamil *kattâlai*. I once had in Mission employ a catechist who was a convert from Brâhmanism, and who was well versed in many of the mysteries of Hinduism. At his request I had a thick iron chain heated till it was red-hot and then suspended by one of its links from the branch of a tree. The catechist had previously smeared his arms and hands with the juice of this aloe; and while the chain was still glowing he ran his hands down it again and again. When I examined them, I found them hot but not in the least injured. If they had not been previously protected by the juice, they would assuredly either have stuck to the hot iron, or have been stripped of every particle of flesh. I think the secret of fire-walking may be found in this direction, though the walkers themselves repudiate the idea, and are perfectly sincere in the performance of what they consider a distinctly religious duty.

DEVIL PROPITIATION.

Devil-worship and devil-dancing, as they are popularly called, are practised every Friday night in almost every village of the Tinnevelly district, where the Shânâr caste reside. The devil-dancer, who is himself a Shânân, dances round a great fire, while the people stand round in a circle. No Englishman is on any account allowed to witness this dance. I once saw the commencement of one from a distance when on horseback, but the moment I was seen the dance stopped at once. The following description is from the pen of Bishop Caldwell, who worked in Tinnevelly for fifty-three years, and who probably knew more of the Shânâr caste than anyone else of his time:—

"The Shânârs are chiefly palmyra-tree cultivators, and farmers, belonging to the Tamil aboriginal race, they have retained their distinct manners and customs and their ancient religion is devil-worship. The majority of the devils are supposed to have been human beings—mostly those who have met with violent or sudden deaths, especially if they have been objects of dread in their lifetime. Devils may be either male or female, low or high caste, of Hindu or foreign lineage. The majority dwell in trees, but some wander to and fro, or take up their abode in the temples erected to their honour, or in houses, and often a person will become possessed. Every evil and misfortune is attributed to demons. Always malignant, never merciful

—inflicting evils, not conferring benefits—their wrath must be appeased, not their favour supplicated. A heap of earth, adorned with white-wash and red ochre, near a large untrimmed tree, constitutes in most cases both the temple and the demons in it, and a smaller heap in front of the temple forms the altar. The tree is supposed to be the devil's ordinary dwelling-place, from which he snuffs up the odour of the sacrificial blood and descends unseen to join the feast. This mode of worship has no particular order of priests. Anyone may be a 'devil-dancer,' as the officiating priest is styled, and who for the occasion is dressed in the vestments of the devil to be worshipped, on which are hideous representations of demons. Thus decorated, amidst the blaze of torches, and accompanied by frightful sounds, the devil-dancer begins his labour. The 'music' is at first comparatively slow, and the dancer seems impassive or sullen, but as it quickens and becomes louder, his excitement rises. Sometimes to work himself into a frenzy, he uses medicated draughts, cuts, lacerates and burns his flesh, drinks the blood flowing from his own wounds, or from the sacrifice, then brandishing his staff of bells, dances with a quick and wild step. Suddenly the afflatus descends; he snorts, stares, and gyrates; the demon has now taken bodily possession of him, and though he retains the power of utterance and motion, both are under the demon's control. The bystanders signalize the event by a long shout, and a peculiar vibratory noise, caused by the hand and tongue. All hasten to consult him as a present deity. As he acts the part of a maniac, it is difficult to interpret his replies, but the wishes of the inquirers generally help them to the answers. The night is the time usually devoted to these orgies, and as the number of devils worshipped is in some districts equal to the number of the worshippers, and as every act is accompanied by the din of drums and the bray of horns, the stillness of the hour is frequently broken by a dismal uproar."[1]

THE RELIGION OF THIEVES.

In England one does not look for much profession of religion from burglars and cattle-lifters, but in India the thief caste is just as religious as any other. To steal is an honourable profession, but to break caste by submitting to baptism is the most dishonourable thing that can be conceived. In the Trichinopoly district the Kalla caste (the chief division of the thief caste) is particularly strong, and is regarded by the other Sûdra castes as quite a respectable community. What I state below I took down in substance from one of their leading men, who had suffered very considerable persecution on being baptized.[2]

The chief temple of the Kallans is about ten miles west of Madura, and is dedicated to Alagarswâmi, said to be an incarnation of Vishnu, but also said to be the

[1] *Two Hundred Years of the S.P.G.*, p. 523.

[2] I have quoted this article as I wrote it for *The Castes and Tribes of South India*, by Mr. E. Thurston, vol. III, 1909.

brother of Mînâtchi (the "fish-eyed," or beautiful daughter of the Pândya king of Madura). Now Mînâtchi has been married by the Brâhmans to Siva, and so we see Hinduism wedded to Drâvidianism, and the spirit of compromise, the chief method of conversion adopted by the Brâhmans, carried to its utmost limit. At the great annual festival the idol of Alagarswâmi is carried in the month of Chittra (April-May) to the temple of Mînâtchi; and the banks of the river Vaiga swarm with two or three lakhs (hundred thousand) of worshippers, a large proportion of whom are Kallans. At this festival the Kallans have the right of dragging with a rope the car of Alagarswâmi, though other people may join in later on. As Alagarswâmi is a vegetarian, no blood sacrifice is offered to him. This is probably due to the influence of Brâhmanism, for, in their ordinary ceremonies, the Kallans invariably slaughter sheep as sacrifices to propitiate their deities. True to their bold and thievish instincts, the Kallans do not hesitate to steal a god, if they think he will be useful to them in their predatory excursions, and are not afraid to dig up the coins or jewels that are generally buried under an idol.[1] Though they entertain little dread of their own village gods, they are often afraid of others that they meet far from home, or in the jungles when they are engaged in one of their stealing expeditions. As regards their own village gods, there is a sort of understanding that, if they help them in their thefts, they are to have a fair

[1] Compare the theft of Laban's teraphim by Rachel (Gen. XXXI. 19).

share of the spoil, and, on the principle of honesty among thieves, the bargain is always kept. At the annual festival for the village deities, each family sacrifices a sheep, and the head of the victim is given to the *pûjâri*, while the body is taken home by the donor, and partaken of as a communion feast. Two at least of the elements of totem worship appear here: there is the shedding of the sacrificial blood of an innocent victim to appease the wrath of the totem god, and the common feasting together which follows it.

When strange deities are met with by the Kallans on their thieving expeditions, it is usual to make a vow that, if the adventure turns out well, part of the spoil shall next day be left at the shrine of the god, or be handed over to the *pûjâri* of that particular deity. They are afraid that if this precaution be not taken, the god may make them blind, or cause them to be discovered, or may go so far as to knock them down and leave them to bleed to death. If they have seen the deity, or been particularly frightened or otherwise specially affected by these unknown gods, instead of leaving a part of the body sacrificed, they adopt a more thorough method of satisfying the angry deity. After a few days they return at midnight to make a special sacrifice, which of course is conducted by the particular *pûjâri* whose god is to be appeased. They bring a sheep with rice, curry-stuffs and liquors, and after the sacrifice give a considerable share of these dainties, together with the animal's head, to the *pûjâri*, as well as a sum of money for making the *pûja* (worship) for them.

Some of the ceremonies that take place at a sacrifice are worth recording. First, the idol is washed in water, and a spot of sandal paste is put on the forehead in the case of male deities, and a spot of *kunkuma* (red powder) in the case of females. Garlands are placed round its neck, and a bell is rung, while lamps are lighted all round. Then the deity's name is repeatedly invoked, accompanied by beating on the *udukku*. This is a small drum which tapers to a narrow waist in the middle, and is held in the left hand of the *pûjâri* with one end close to his left ear, while he taps on it with the fingers of his right hand. Not only is this primitive music pleasing to the ears of his barbarous audience, but, what is more important, it conveys the oracular communications of the god himself. By means of the end of the drum placed close to his ear, the *pûjâri* is enabled to hear what the god has to say of the predatory excursion which has taken place; and the *pûjâri*—who like a clever gipsy has taken care previously to get as much information as possible—retails all that has occurred during the exploit to his wondering devotees. In case his information is incomplete, he is easily able to find out, by a few leading questions and a little cross-examination of these ignorant people, all that he needs to impress them with the idea that the god knows all about their transactions, having been present at their plundering bout.

At all such sacrifices, it is a common custom to pour

a little water over the sheep, to see if it will shake itself, this being invariably a sign of the deity's acceptance of the animal offered. If the sheep does not shake itself, it is rejected, and another substituted for it; and in some cases—be it whispered—when the *pûjâri* thinks the sheep too thin and scraggy, he pours over it only a little water, which the sheep ignores, and so he demands another animal. If, however, the *pûjâri*, as the god's representative, is satisfied, he goes on pouring more and more water till the half-drenched animal has to shake itself, and so sign its own death-warrant. It is essential that the head should be struck off with one blow of the knife. All who have ventured forth in the night to take part in the sacrifice then join in the communal meal.

An illustration of the value of sacrifices compared with the small value attaching to an oath made in the presence of a god, may here be given. Some servants of a Kallan land-owner one day stole a sheep, for which they were brought up before the village munsif, or magistrate. When they denied the theft, the munsif took them to their village god, Karuppan (the black brother), and made them swear in its presence. They perjured themselves again, and were let off. Their master quietly questioned them afterwards, asking how they dared to swear so falsely before their own god, and to this they replied, "While we were swearing, we were mentally offering a sacrifice of a sheep to him" —which they subsequently carried out—to pacify him for the double crime of stealing and perjury.

. . . .

Enough proof has now been given, I trust, to show that the religion of the lower and illiterate castes of the villages is a totally different thing from that of the orthodox Hindus of the towns. They are different in essence as well as in motive, different in the object of worship or of dread, and different in their practice. It is not an adequate answer to say that these lower castes often attend the festivals at the large temples where the higher Hinduism prevails; that they sing songs from the great epics, or act dramas taken from the Mahâbhârata. Nor is it sufficient to argue that they all call themselves Hindus, and all keep caste; for the two systems stand on different foundations. There is one trait, however, besides caste, which is common to all Hindus—and a very admirable trait it is—their love of religion. Perhaps the dread of evil spirits and cruel goddesses ought not to be dignified by such an honourable term as "religion"; but, at any rate, such a thing as atheism, as we understand the word, may be said to be almost unknown in India. At the recent census of 1911, out of a total population of 315,000,000 only seventeen entered themselves as avowed "atheists". When everything is prosperous the ordinary Hindu may be careless and apathetic, but when cholera is rife, famine grips him, or when the festival comes round, he is filled with religious enthusiasm.

In Chapter VI I quoted the remark of a writer on Hinduism that, "In each of its stages the core of the religion is really Pantheistic". In my own mind I have not the least doubt that the core of Hinduism is really sacrifice. We find that in the first period the Âryans joined with the pre-Âryans in their sacrifices. During the Vêdic period all India was drenched with sacrificial blood, more so even than Palestine under the Israelites. There were practised, beside all minor sacrifices, the *rishaba mêdha*, the bull sacrifice, the *asva mêdha*, the horse sacrifice, and also the *nara mêdha*, or human sacrifice. With the rise of Buddhism and the growth of the doctrine of transmigration the blood-sacrifice naturally died out among the descendants of the Âryans, i.e. the Brâhmans and Râjputs. But it is quite clear that however much the philosophy of the Brâhmans has overshadowed the whole country, and however wide the border-land between the two systems, the religion of the Drâvidians always was, as it now is, based on sacrifice. Even in the higher Hinduism we have the cult of Prajâpathi, the "Lord of Creatures," half mortal and half immortal, who sacrificed himself, and made all other sacrifices symbolical of his own. Sacrifice was spoken of as "a good ferrying boat for getting over the ocean of sin"; and here, if only for a moment, Hinduism gets into closer touch with the Incarnation than at any other time.

This phase of the real religion of India carries us back to an age so dim and hoary as to be lost in oblivion. It is worthy of note that the aboriginal races of India have never tended to die out like those of Australia or the Maoris of New Zealand, and also that the spirit of sacrifice has persisted in spite of the prevailing influence of the higher Hinduism and the onslaughts of Buddhism. Can we not trace here a consciousness of sin, in the real sense of the word, and a yearning for forgiveness, however much the idea has been distorted and obscured? The meaning of many of the sacrificial rites, such as the pouring of water on the victim, the mixing of the blood and rice, the placing of the right foreleg of the slain animal in its mouth, and the smearing of its face with the fat of the entrails, etc., seems to have disappeared entirely during the lapse of all these centuries; but certain other practices seem to bring us into touch with vital doctrines. As in totemism all over the uncivilized world—with which this sacrificial system seems undoubtedly to be associated—there are certain prominent features common to all. The blood of the victim is spilled on the ground, and man admits his guilt, by means of transmission to the innocent animal, in the presence of the offended deity. In the Meriah sacrifice the human being was *bought* for so much money, so that the sin of murder should not be added to the other crimes. And while the youth is dying the assembled multitude dance around to music, and addressing the earth say: "O God, we offer the sacrifice to you. Give us good crops, seasons, and health." After which they address the victim: "We bought you with a price, and did not seize you. Now we sacrifice you according to custom, and no sin rests with us."[1] In many sacrifices the officiating *pûjâri* dips his finger in the hot blood, and with it marks his forehead; then all who participate in the sacri-

[1] *Ethnographic Notes*, p. 512.

fice do the same. This is the sacred blood-bond, which unites all the tribe, caste, or community into one united brotherhood. It is also the way in which new members of a community are initiated, and become associated with the confraternity. Then again, the body of the sacrificed animal is eaten together by those who offer the sacrifice. This is the communion, which not only seals the friendship of man with his brother, but unites man with his now reconciled God, and God with the now pardoned sinner.

There is only one doctrine that can cover all these conflicting beliefs, and can meet the spiritual needs of all these poor, benighted people; but that one central doctrine of the Incarnation covers and satisfies them all. There is always a tendency either to make incarnations on the Nestorian or Vaishnavite model of God being temporarily associated with a man or an animal, or else by elevating some creature of the earth into a god. This is at the root of idolatry. It is natural that some material object should be looked upon as the embodiment of the Supreme. Wherever there is a pantheistic conception, then a stone is god because everything is god, and it is easier to worship a stone that one can see than an abstract spirit that the eye cannot see or the mind comprehend. And with idolatry, which is common to the whole world, there is also found a dread of devils and evil spirits, a deification of nature and anthropomorphic conceptions of the Deity. Where these do not exist there is nothing left but rank materialism, which is the direct antithesis of pantheism, since there is no room for the Infinite where everything is finite. So the child-races of the world are always inclined to turn their heroes into gods; to propitiate the spirits of those who have met with strange or violent deaths; to appease the anger of their gods and goddesses with sacrifices; to find gods in stocks and stones, in beasts, birds, and snakes; to look upon their devil-dancers and medicine-men as representatives of God on earth; and to expect and invent incarnations in response to the demand for them. Thus men and animals, spirits good and bad, are elevated into deities, by a kind of incarnation reaching from below upwards. Such ideas, I repeat, are common to all heathendom in some shape or other. As Pope said of the West Indian :—

> " Lo the poor Indian, whose untutored mind
> Sees God in cloud, and hears Him in the wind,
> And thinks, admitted to that equal sky,
> His faithful dog shall bear him company ".
>
> (*Essay on Man.*)

The Incarnate Son, the Image of the invisible God, is the Saviour towards Whom all these blind hands have been unconsciously groping and stretching in all ages and in all countries. Since God became Man, idolatry has become an impossibility. God in human form is the object and complete fulfilment of man's adoration. All pagan ideas are taken up, purified and deified in the personality of Jesus Christ. I cannot do better than sum up my argument in the words of a friend:—[1]

"No Nestorian conception of a human personality with which Deity associates itself gives the Gospel truth. The Lord of Glory did not become—could not have become—'one of us,' but He stooped to recapitulate and sum up in Himself all humanity in its unfallen and ideal verity. He was not made 'a man' —a thing impossible—but Man. Such is the universality of the Christian message—all men are become brothers in Christ the catholic Man, Whose birth is the 'touch of nature,' which not merely appeals to human sympathies, but 'makes all men kin'. But yet again, that which took our poor nature was supernature. Attempts to resolve the story of redeemed humanity into an evolutionary working upwards of the immanent divinity residing in the race may achieve a kind of theism not far removed from pantheism; but they cannot be accepted by Christian believers. The Incarnation was not the crown and flower of human development, but the entrance of the Most High into human conditions, for deliverance and healing. Christianity stands, not merely for the divine, but for the supernatural, the invasion of the natural order by redemptive and curative forces from the kingdom of grace. From heaven He came and sought us, and angels from the realm of glory, who heralded the wondrous Birth, are His ministers to succour and defend men on earth."

[1] Canon Douglas Macleane.

The Hindu sages have dreamed and striven and strained, as never men have striven before, to fix a ladder on earth which shall reach up to heaven and bring them to the golden feet of the Ineffable. In this they resembled the poet who reared his beautiful palace of music, "built," as he sings, "broad on the roots of things" in earth to scale the vault of heaven with its "rampired walls of gold as transparent as glass". But as the sages' feet failed to climb the steep ascent, so the poet's palace failed to rise up to heaven, until "the emulous heaven yearned down, made effort to reach the earth". For by no possible means can man ever reach God, till God reaches down to man. When the Son of God, "to match man's birth," was Himself born in the flesh, then heaven was brought down to earth, the Word became Man; and so God and man, heaven and earth became united in one embrace, and henceforth there was "no more near nor far". The poet called the keys of his organ to their work, claiming each slave of sound—"armies of angels that war, legions of demons that lurk"—and bade them "pile him a palace straight," till he fancied that the unseen heights were about to be scaled and heaven won:—

"For higher still and higher . . .
Up, the pinnacled glory reached, and the pride of my
soul was in sight.
In sight? Not half! for it seemed, it was certain, to
match man's birth,

Nature in turn conceived, obeying an impulse as I;
And the emulous heaven yearned down, made effort to reach the earth,
As the earth had done her best, in my passion, to scale the sky:
Novel splendours burst forth, grew familiar and dwelt with mine,
Not a point nor peak but found, and fixed its wandering star;
Meteor-moons, balls of blaze: and they did not pale nor pine,
For earth had attained to heaven, there was no more near nor far."

(*Abt Vogler*, Browning.)

INDEX.